UNDERSTAND

Also in this series:

UNDERSTANDING TAROT

A practical guide to Tarot card reading

by

Jocelyn Almond & Keith Seddon

Thorsons

An Imprint of HarperCollins*Publishers*

Thorsons
An Imprint of HarperCollins*Publishers*
77–85 Fulham Palace Road,
Hammersmith, London W6 8JB
1160 Battery Street
San Francisco, California 94111–1213

First published by Aquarian 1991
Thorsons edition 1995
7 9 10 8 6

A catalogue record for this book
is available from the British Library

ISBN 1 85538 087 0

Typeset by G&M, Raunds, Northamptonshire
Printed and bound in Great Britain by
Caledonian International Book Manufacturing Ltd, Glasgow

ACKNOWLEDGEMENTS

The Tarot cards on pages 27 and 34 are reproduced by kind permission of Eddison Sadd Editions and are from *The Mythic Tarot* pack of cards and book by Juliet Sharman-Burke and Liz Green, published in the UK by Rider (Random Century), in the USA by Simon & Schuster, in Canada by Stoddart (General Publishing), in Australia by Collins, Angus & Robertson, in Germany by Hugendubel, in Italy by Armenia, in France by Solar, in Portugal by Siciliano, in Spain by Edaf and in Greece by Oceanida.

The illustration from *Crowley's Thoth Tarot* reproduced by permission of U.S. Games Systems, Inc., Stamford, CT 06902 USA. ©1978, 1983 by Stuart R. Kaplan and Donald Weiser. Further reproduction prohibited.

The illustration from the *Motherpeace Round Tarot* deck reproduced by permission of U.S. Games Systems, Inc., Stamford, CT 06902 USA. ©1981, 1983 by Motherpeace Round Tarot. Further reproduction prohibited.

Illustrations from the *Barbara Walker Tarot* deck reproduced by permission of U.S. Games Systems, Inc., Stamford, CT 06902

CONTENTS

INTRODUCTION

This book shows you how to use Tarot cards for divination, or what is commonly called fortune-telling. Although in many respects it is an introductory book, giving instructions which the complete beginner can follow, it is also designed to be a handy reference book for more experienced Tarot readers.

The Tarot is one of the most popular and easy-to-use systems of divination because it does not require unusual psychic gifts. Even the most inexperienced reader can obtain surprisingly good results right from the start, and it is possible to make swift progress if one's skills are practised regularly.

A further advantage is that Tarot reading is free of the dangers involved in certain occult activities in which special training is required, without which the practitioner might be exposed to a risk of psychic or mental disturbance. In contrast to this, Tarot does not depend upon invoking spirits or unleashing supernatural forces; instead, the user of Tarot learns to be more intuitive and open to the impressions coming from the unconscious mind. We all naturally have this ability, which manifests itself from time to time in the form of precognitive dreams, strange feelings or forebodings, impressions about people we meet, or the sense that someone we know needs our help, but unfortunately we often tend to disregard such experiences and think it irrational to rely upon them. Tarot reading is a way of gaining greater control over this intuitive capacity so that it can be called upon when needed to provide guidance.

History of the Tarot

It is not known exactly when or where Tarot cards originated, though there has been much speculation, with claims for their having come from Egypt, China, Persia or India. Certainly there were playing cards in China and India before they were known in Europe, but they differed from the earliest European cards, and there is no evidence of a direct influence. One theory is that they were brought to Europe by the gypsies, but though gypsies used cards for fortune-telling, it is unlikely that they invented them, or that they brought them from their country of origin, India (though at one time gypsies were wrongly believed to have come from Egypt, hence their name).

Another theory is that the Tarot was named after the River Taro, which is a tributary of the River Po in northern Italy, and that the cards were invented near there.

An entry dated 1392 in the ledger of King Charles VI of France records that a painter called Jacquemin Gringonneur made three packs of coloured and gilded playing cards for the king. Other references to playing cards earlier in the fourteenth century suggest that they became popular in Europe at about this time. However, it is not clear whether these early references were to Tarot cards as we know them today or to some other kind of playing cards.

There are several types of early Tarot pack. Modern Tarot decks, which have 78 cards, are based on the Venetian or Piedmontese Tarot. There was a different, 97-card deck, now known as the Florentine Tarot or minchiate, which included cards representing the signs of the zodiac, the four elements and four extra virtues which do not appear in modern standard decks. There was also the

Bolognese Tarot, called the tarochinno (which means 'little Tarot deck', because it had only 62 cards). Furthermore, there were variations between different standard versions, especially in the numbering of the Major Arcana or Trump cards.

In the fifteenth century, several packs of Tarot cards were painted for the Visconti-Sforza family of Milan, one of which is a standard 78-card deck of which 74 cards have survived and are now in museums and private collections. It is evidence that many of the traditional Tarot images have changed very little from then until the present day.

Tarot cards were probably originally used for playing games, but many of the early references show that the Church tended to disapprove of the Tarot and suspected it of containing some anti-Christian or subversive message; so even from the earliest times the cards may have been used for divination, and were certainly thought by some people to bear pagan images.

It was not until the eighteenth century, however, that a serious attempt was made to connect the Tarot systematically with ancient pagan esoteric beliefs. In 1781, an archaeologist and amateur scholar of the occult, Antoine Court de Gébelin, published the eighth volume of his enormous work *Le Monde Primitif.* It contained a section on the Tarot, in which he put forward his idea that the cards were a remnant of an ancient Egyptian book of magic, called the *Book of Thoth*, and had been brought by the gypsies from Egypt. He was also the first to suggest that there was a connection between the cards of the Tarot's Major Arcana and the letters of the Hebrew alphabet — an idea taken up by many subsequent commentators on the Tarot.

Court de Gébelin's theory was later developed by Alliette, a hairdresser and professional fortune-teller. He connected the Tarot to the Hebrew mystical system of the Cabala, and devised his own 'rectified' version of the Tarot which he believed was more faithful to its presumed ancient origins.

In the nineteenth century, Eliphas Lévi further advanced these ideas of a connection between the Cabala and the Tarot, and his views have had a powerful influence over the way in which Tarot has been understood ever since. The theory that it is the *Book of*

Thoth and that it has correspondences with the Cabala became generally accepted by nineteenth-century commentators and firmly incorporated into Tarot tradition.

Finally, a major influence upon the way in which the cards are used and the meanings most usually ascribed to them today comes from the Hermetic Order of the Golden Dawn. This was an esoteric society founded in 1888 and which included a number of famous people among its members, such as W. B. Yeats and Bram Stoker. According to the Golden Dawn, astrology, alchemy, divination, numerology, the Cabala and ritual magic were all aspects of a single esoteric system to which the Tarot was the central key.

The society followed Lévi's teaching on the Tarot, but the order of correspondence between the letters of the Hebrew alphabet and the cards of the Major Arcana was altered, and the cards of Justice and Strength were transposed in the numbered sequence, for reasons explained later in this book.

Two of the Golden Dawn's members were A. E. Waite and Pamela Colman Smith, who designed the famous Rider-Waite Tarot. This deck, and Waite's book, *The Pictorial Key to the Tarot*, published in 1910, have been extremely influential. Many modern decks are based on the Rider-Waite, and most modern books on the Tarot (including this one) contain meanings for the cards which are derived to a greater or lesser extent from Waite's meanings (which in turn were based on those used by the Golden Dawn).

Aleister Crowley was another member who later achieved fame in his own right. His book on the Tarot, called *The Book of Thoth* (published in 1944 in a limited edition), and the deck designed by him and painted by Lady Frieda Harris, have also influenced later writers and artists, and made an important contribution to the growing Tarot tradition.

Since the early 1970s, interest in the Tarot has increased, and many new decks have been designed, some of which are new interpretations of the traditional themes, others being based on themes inspired by various different cultures, mythologies and esoteric or divinatory systems.

INTRODUCTION

Uses of the Tarot

The use of Tarot cards with which people are most familiar is divination. This does not necessarily mean predicting the future, although some degree of prediction is usually involved. The simpler forms of fortune-telling are often treated as a sort of game or entertainment — something which is done for fun at parties. There is probably no harm in this approach, but on the other hand, very little good may come of it either. There is, of course, a slight danger that sensitive people may take to heart 'predictions' made for them in a spirit of fun, when these may be unreliable in such circumstances.

We are assuming that readers of this book want to take a more serious approach, using the Tarot to seek guidance when problems and difficult decisions are faced. The Tarot cannot always provide answers, and because it is dependent upon both the interpretation of the reader and the state of mind of the person who has come for the reading, it certainly should not be thought of as infallible or regarded with superstitious reverence. However, it is helpful in clarifying thoughts, bringing feelings into the open, as well as suggesting ideas and possibilities which may not previously have been considered.

When doing a Tarot reading for a friend, the cards provide a kind of neutral zone in which it becomes possible to discuss issues which might otherwise seem too personal or embarrassing. At the same time, any advice given is fairly free from the emotional involvement and bias of opinion which is otherwise inevitable when one is trying to help a friend. Because guidance is suggested by cards which have been chosen at random from a shuffled pack, the advice given is not simply the personal opinion of the reader.

It is also possible to read the cards for oneself. Sometimes it is said that this is bad luck, but there is really no basis for thinking so. The only difficulty which arises is that one may be so enmeshed in one's personal problems that it becomes hard to interpret the cards in a relaxed and unprejudiced manner; there may be a tendency to impose upon the cards an interpretation which is desired, rather than one which is true and reliable. The most successful readings done for oneself are less a way of predicting the future and more like a form of meditation, because knowledge of the Tarot enables the reader to reflect upon the deeper meanings and associations of the cards which would probably not be mentioned when doing a reading for someone else.

In the main part of this book, we show you how to do Tarot readings for yourself and your friends. There are other uses of the Tarot, however, and we discuss these briefly in the final chapter. The cards may be used as an aid to meditation, they may be employed during certain types of counselling or therapy, when working in a group or engaging in ritual practices, or as an inspiration for story-telling — and they can, of course, still be used simply for playing games.

CHAPTER ONE

STRUCTURE AND ATTRIBUTIONS OF THE TAROT

Choosing your deck and getting to know it

Before we start to look at how to use the Tarot cards, it seems sensible to give some advice on the points you need to consider when deciding which deck, out of the vast number available, is most suitable for your purposes. If you have not yet got any Tarot cards, we hope this advice will be useful to you. On the other hand, we realise that many people are reading this book because they have already bought a Tarot deck or have received one as a gift; but in the course of time most students of the Tarot acquire a small collection, so even if you have a deck already, similarly we hope this advice will be useful if you wish to buy another.

We know from experience as teachers of Tarot that, unfortunately, sometimes people start learning with a deck which is not suitable for their needs and does not appeal to their personal tastes, which can cause problems. It is worthwhile, therefore, taking time and care to choose a Tarot deck which you really like, because you will do better readings with it. There is a wide selection available from specialist occult outlets, mail order suppliers, and from some bookshops, and you should be able to see samples of cards before you make your choice of which to buy.

It is very important to use a Tarot deck which is your own — not a second-hand one or one borrowed from someone else. This is because all objects have a distinctive atmosphere about them which is detectable by sensitive people; in fact, the history of an object and its ownership can be sensed by people who have developed this skill which is called psychometry. Therefore, if you wish to use an object — in this instance, a Tarot deck — in developing your own psychic skills it is not a good idea to use one which has already become imbued with another person's psychic vibrations, because you want to make it personal to you.

In the case of Tarot cards, you are going to be using a device which is supposed to stimulate your own unconscious impressions and amplify latent psychic ability by means of evocative pictures, so it is also important that you choose a pack of cards which looks attractive to you and which arouses your imagination.

For beginners, it is best to use a fully pictorial Tarot — that is, one with pictures on the Pip cards of the Minor Arcana. Traditional decks designed before the twentieth century have only the suit symbols on the Pip cards, like ordinary playing cards, and it is very difficult to remember the meanings attached to these cards when they all look so similar, whereas distinctive pictures stimulate your memory and your imagination.

Whenever you get a new Tarot pack you should spend some time studying the pictures on the cards before you start doing readings with them. This is particularly important if you are completely new to the Tarot. Tarot images are not like illustrations in a book, where the written text tells you what they are about, or like pictures which are hung up for decoration and which are to be appreciated at face value or for their aesthetic qualities. Tarot images are symbolic, and each feature of the image may have a meaning attached to it, so it is important to discover why the artist or designer of the deck you are using has decided to include that particular imagery. Often, this will be explained in a book or leaflet accompanying the cards, while the more common and traditional symbolism is usually explained in any good book on the Tarot.

The more that you use the cards, the more you will find yourself relying upon the pictures on the cards rather than upon meanings you have read in books, and the pictures will begin to suggest to you personal interpretations which you may not have read about anywhere. Extensions of meanings, or subtle nuances of meanings which you have read, will come to mind as you examine the pictures and see new ways of interpreting them.

Finally, when you are a newcomer to Tarot, it is important to start with a standard 78-card deck (explained in the next section), and not one of the fortune-telling card packs which are based on the Tarot but which have names, numbering and images which do not conform to tradition. Once you have learnt how to use the Tarot, it is easy to adapt to using a non-standard deck which has been derived from the traditional Tarot. It is, however far more difficult to make the transition the other way round, or from one non-standard Tarot to a different non-standard Tarot if you do not already understand the tradition from which they have developed.

Structure of the standard Tarot

In medieval times there were several versions of the Tarot. The one we know today as the standard Tarot deck is based on an Italian form known as the Venetian or Piedmontese Tarot which had become the standard version in Italy by the beginning of the sixteenth century.

There are 78 cards in the deck, which is divided into two parts: the Major Arcana or Trumps, and the Minor Arcana. (The word 'Arcana' means mysteries or secrets.)

The Minor Arcana consists of 56 cards divided into four suits, each suit having ten Pip cards and four Court cards. Apart from the extra Court card in each suit (the Knight), the Minor Arcana resembles a pack of modern playing cards, but the suits have different names: Wands, Rods or Batons (corresponding to Clubs); Cups (corresponding to Hearts); Swords (corresponding to Spades); and Coins, Pentacles or Discs (corresponding to Diamonds). The

Court cards are traditionally called King, Queen, Knight and Page, but some decks use different names. This is explained in Chapter 5, which deals with the Court cards in detail.

It is the Major Arcana which makes the Tarot interesting, because of its mysterious and esoteric imagery which seems to contain influences from ancient pagan traditions. The 22 cards of the Major Arcana form a sequence of 21 numbered cards, plus one unnumbered card called The Fool (although this is sometimes numbered zero). They depict strange scenes and male and female figures which appear to be of allegorical significance. Theories about the symbolism in these pictures have proliferated, so that many modern packs have designs which emphasise this symbolism and elaborate upon it, often including the idiosyncratic interpretations of a particular artist or designer. We explain more about this in Chapter 3, where the most common symbolism is described, along with the divinatory meanings of the cards.

There is a traditional order to the sequence of cards in the Major Arcana, but some decks deviate from this. The most common change is to transpose the cards of Justice and Strength. This occurs in the Rider-Waite deck and those based on it. The reason for this is explained in Chapter 3, under the sections for the relevant cards. In some decks also, some of the cards have been given different names. Because we intend this book to be used with any standard deck, we mention the most commonly occurring alternative names, and those which appear on famous or popular decks, in the sections dealing with those cards, but of course it is impossible to take account of all the variations. If you are using cards which have alternative names and numbering, to avoid confusion it may be helpful to make a note of the different names or numbers in the margins of this book, alongside the relevant sections.

Attributions of the symbols

To the newcomer to Tarot, it can sometimes seem as if each card has a divinatory meaning ascribed to it on a quite arbitrary basis.

One can be inclined to feel this especially when looking at a list of meanings in the leaflet accompanying the cards, and when referring to certain simplistic books on the Tarot which say little more than the leaflets. Taking this view can make it difficult to remember the meanings, as one meaning might seem as good as another for any individual card.

Another difficulty, of an opposite nature, is that some books on the Tarot are very complicated, connecting the Tarot to astrology, the Hebrew Cabala, and other esoteric systems. These correlations are of interest to the more advanced practitioner, but can be daunting to the learner. You may be using a deck which has astrological symbols on it, letters of the Hebrew alphabet, runes, colours which have a symbolic significance, and so on, but if you are a beginner, it is quite unnecessary to study all this before starting to use the cards for divination.

However, some basic understanding of the underlying philosophy and system of attributions which has become attached to the Tarot over the years is necessary in order to understand why the cards have acquired the divinatory meanings which are commonly given to them today. We shall therefore be looking at the three most important themes which enable you to do this: gender, numbers and elements.

The meaning of each card in the Minor Arcana takes into account the meaning associated with the element ascribed to each suit together with (in the case of a Pip card) its number, or (in the case of a Court card) its gender. For many cards of the Major Arcana the meaning is related to the card's gender, and some commentators again see a significance in the number of each card (though in this book we shall not be examining the meaning of numbers in the Major Arcana, for reasons explained later). All this may sound rather confusing at the moment, but it will become clearer as we take each of the three themes in turn.

Gender

According to ancient beliefs, there are two equal, opposite, but complementary principles at work in the universe — a feminine principle and a masculine principle. In Chinese philosophy they are called yin and yang. The gods, goddesses, heroes and heroines in mythology may be seen as embodiments of various aspects of these principles.

The feminine principle is associated with the moon, night, the natural world, feeling and emotion, the unconscious mind, the underworld of the dead, introversion, and passive, nurturing qualities. Sometimes it is thought of as negative, dark or destructive, although one of its important aspects is the female creative capacity for giving birth to new life.

The masculine principle is associated with the sun, daylight, the conscious mind, rational thinking, extroversion, and the power and authority which arises from the ego. It is seen as positive, creative and active.

This is not supposed to suggest that men behave solely in accordance with the masculine principle and that women behave solely in accordance with the feminine principle: the terms 'masculine' and 'feminine' are ways of characterising these equal but opposite forces. A psychologically well-balanced individual possesses both masculine and feminine traits, and much of the philosophy of the Tarot is concerned with reconciling these opposites and achieving harmonious union between them.

Many cards of the Major Arcana represent aspects of either the masculine or the feminine principle. The card of The Sun, for instance, is masculine; the card of The Moon is feminine. The Magician and The Emperor personify aspects of the masculine principle, while The High Priestess and The Empress personify aspects of the feminine principle. The Chariot and Temperance, on the other hand, show interaction between these opposing principles, and The World represents an ideal condition transcending the duality of gender.

In the Minor Arcana, the suits of Wands and Swords are masculine, the suit symbols being phallic objects. The suits of Cups and Coins are feminine, the circular or container form of their symbols representing the womb. Numbers are also conceived of as masculine or feminine, as are the four elements, and of course the Court cards of the Minor Arcana depict male and female characters, so we have to take account of gender in these respects as well.

Numbers

It has long been believed that numbers have a meaning, or a magical or mystical significance. The ancient Jews believed this, as can be seen by the importance given to numbers and measurements in the Bible. The Greek mathematician Pythagoras also thought that they had a mystical quality. Even if we have not studied numerology, we are all aware to some extent of numbers possessing meaning. We know, for instance, that the number three is often regarded as lucky and that thirteen is supposed to be unlucky.

The meanings attributed to the cards of the Tarot's Minor Arcana depend to a large extent upon the meaning of each card's number. The meaning of each number is then qualified according to the attributes of the suit to which the card belongs. For example, the meaning of the Four of Wands is determined by the meaning of the number four together with the meaning attached to the suit of Wands as a whole (which is determined by the element associated with each suit, as explained below).

The cards of the Major Arcana are also numbered, and some commentators have explored the significance of these numbers with regard to the meanings of the Major Arcana; however, we shall not do that in this book, for two reasons. Firstly, early Tarot decks do not carry numbers on the cards of the Major Arcana, and originally the sequence of these cards was not generally agreed upon; therefore the cards of the Major Arcana were recognisable and meaningful regardless of their numbering. Secondly, because the Major Arcana can be adequately understood without analysing its numbers, we do not want to complicate matters by exploring that aspect of the Tarot here.

The meaning attached to each number in the Minor Arcana is explained in Chapter 4, where we have grouped the Pip cards according to number rather than suit so that the significance of the numbering can be more readily seen.

Elements

It used to be thought that the physical world was composed of four basic elements, and that all substances were made from the combination of these elements in varying quantities. This idea originated in ancient Greek philosophy. The four elements were fire, water, air and earth, and they were believed not only to compose inanimate physical objects but also to determine the psychological as well as the physical constitution of human beings.

Fire and air are conceived of as masculine elements, while water and earth are feminine. The qualities of the masculine and feminine principles, as described above, therefore apply to the elements.

Each suit of the Tarot's Minor Arcana has one of the four elements attributed to it. The suit of Wands is associated with fire, Cups with water, Swords with air, and Coins with earth; so the meanings of the cards in each suit are determined by the qualities associated with the element attributed to the suit in question. The Court cards represent people, and the personality traits of these individuals are again based on the qualities of the element attached to each suit.

However, the elements, (or humours, as they are called in a psychological context) relate to the Court cards in another way as well. The King of each suit has the element of air attributed to it, while the Queens are associated with water, the Knights with fire, and the Pages with earth. Thus, the personality of the Page of Wands is determined by a combination of the properties of fire (the element attributed to the the suit of Wands) and the properties of earth (the element attributed to the Page of each suit). Likewise, the personality of the Knight of Cups is made up of a combination of water (for the suit of Cups) and fire (because he is a Knight). You can see for yourself that, according to this system, the Page of Coins has the most earthy character, the Knight of Wands the most fiery, the Queen of Cups the most watery, and the King of Swords the most airy; while the characters of the other cards are formed by a combination of two elements to produce a personality of inner harmony or inner tensions, according to how well those elements mix.

Recognising this basic system of ideas underlying the meanings of the cards in the Minor Arcana may help you to see why each card has its particular meaning. When we examine the Minor Arcana in detail in Chapters 4 and 5, these ideas will become clearer, so do not worry if they sound rather confusing at first.

Learning the meanings of the cards

Learning the divinatory meanings of the cards can appear to be one of the most difficult aspects of learning how to do Tarot card readings. Most books on the Tarot provide both upright and reverse meanings, making 156 meanings in all. Understandably, many amateur Tarot readers make no attempt to learn the meanings, relying upon looking them up in a book instead; but this can render the process of doing a reading laboriously slow, and the sense of what one is saying can be lost because of an inability to relate together the different cards in the spread.

If learning the meanings really were a matter of memorising 156 entirely distinct meanings, it would certainly be a formidable task; but, as we have already shown, this can be simplified by understanding the underlying principles of gender, numbers and elements. This considerably narrows down the amount of memorisation required. In the case of the Minor Arcana, for instance, rather than trying to remember 56 upright and 56 reverse meanings, one can learn the meanings of the four elements and ten numbers (that is, 14 basic meanings) and derive the other meanings from combinations of these basic 14. In Chapters 4 and 5, in which we describe the Minor Arcana, the meanings of the cards are explained in these terms in order to make it clear how each meaning has been derived, so that you can understand and remember it more easily.

However, this is not all that may be done to simplify the learning process. Studying the pictures on the cards, making up stories about them, using Key Words to stimulate the memory, and relating the meanings of the cards to one's personal experience, are all helpful methods which we shall look at now.

The Major Arcana as a Mnemonic Device

A mnemonic device is something which helps you to remember a piece of information. Sometimes it takes the form of a rhyme, such as 'Thirty days hath September'. In music, the sentence 'Every good boy deserves favour' is used to help students to remember the notes on the treble stave. Often, however, symbolic images are used for this purpose of aiding the memory. Medieval stained glass windows, for instance, contain a vast amount of information encoded in their images, and medieval people, most of whom could not read, relied upon such imagery to help them remember teaching from scripture.

Some Tarot commentators have suggested that the Major Arcana is one such mnemonic device. Whether or not it was originally designed for this purpose, the imagery of many modern decks relates to the meaning of each card and can therefore be of help in remembering the divinatory meanings. To benefit from this, you should study the picture on each card in the Tarot deck which you are using, and then read the appropriate meaning in the book, trying to connect the meaning to the picture on your card. After you have read the meaning, look at the picture on the card again and try to recall the meaning. Try to relate each aspect of the meaning to a feature of the picture. If there are symbols in the picture which are intended by the artist or designer to have a particular meaning, you may be able to find out what this is by referring to an accompanying booklet for the deck. On the other hand, many versions of the Tarot use the same symbols, and we have explained the significance of these commonly occurring symbols under the sections for each card in Chapter 3 where we address the Major Arcana.

If you cannot find what a symbol is intended to mean, there is no reason why you should not use it in your own way to stimulate your memory or to give you ideas. It does not matter how you do this; the connections you make between picture and meaning may be entirely personal. For instance, something in the picture may remind you of a personal experience which happens to relate to the divinatory meaning of the card. We shall look at this approach in more detail at the end of this chapter, with regard to learning the meanings of the Court cards. First, however, in order to show more precisely how meaning can be seen in the image on a Major Arcana card we shall examine several versions of one of the cards in the Major Arcana — The Empress.

We have chosen The Empress for this purpose because its central theme — the concept of 'mother' — is fairly simple to use as an example, but at the same time the related meanings are quite diverse, and the symbolism on some versions of this card is complex.

Divinatory meanings of The Empress are love, marriage, childbirth, motherhood, a pleasant environment, happy family life, security and comfort. Emotional well-being and fulfilment, perhaps as a consequence of material security, are also signified.

The Empress (Motherpeace Round Tarot)

In the Motherpeace version of this card, different aspects of the meaning are suggested by four different female figures in the picture. In the middle is a reclining, semi-naked woman draped in a leopardskin and holding a red rose. At her side is a hand mirror. Her pose is reminiscent of nude female figures in art which represent women's erotic nature and are sometimes identified with Venus or Aphrodite. The red rose signifies passion and menstrual blood, relating to the sex and child-bearing aspects of the card's meaning. The mirror stands for 'reflection' in the sense of looking within oneself to gain self-knowledge, reminding us that the meaning of the card is not only concerned with physical comforts but also with a deeper, spiritual satisfaction.

In the top right of the picture is a representation of the Venus of Laussel — a Paleolithic fertility figure in the form of a woman with a horn. The horn is a symbol for abundance, called a horn of plenty, or cornucopia. It stands for the fertility of the earth, a good harvest and plenty to eat and drink.

On the left of the picture is a much later fertility figure from the city of Catal Hüyük: a heavily pregnant woman sitting between two leopards. The leopards are totem animals of Aphrodite, goddess of beauty and love, and the pregnant woman again reminds us that childbirth is one of the meanings attached to this card. However, the woman sits between the leopards as if seated on a throne, and this (as well as the title of the card) suggests a further aspect of the meaning. We should not think of The Empress as representing motherhood in a narrow sense, as much of the card's meaning is about being in a comfortable, orderly, safe environment in which not only are our animal needs provided for, but also where we can develop loving relationships and express our human capacity for creativity in artistic and spiritual ways as well as in the purely physical sense of procreation.

The image of the woman enthroned thus represents the civilised values of a stable society in which people live in well-built homes (rather than travelling around, scavenging for food), and have social institutions such as marriage. This idea is reinforced by the bull in the background of the picture: the keeping and breeding of livestock for food is an important stage in the development of human society, freeing people from the hunter-gatherer subsistence level of existence and providing a more stable and comfortable way of life.

Finally, at the foot of the picture is an image of the Greek earth-mother goddess Demeter, holding ears of wheat, and serpents representing regeneration. As with the other figures, Demeter stands for fertility in a general sense, but the ears of wheat here emphasise the cultivation of food. Even more than the keeping of livestock (which is practised by nomadic tribes as well as by societies which settle in one place), cultivation of the land enabled people to establish a more stable way of life, building towns and cities and developing civilisation in the form of philosophy, art, science and technology. The comfortable standard of living which most people in Western society enjoy today is ultimately dependent upon the cultivation of the fruits of the earth and, as a whole, the card of The Empress symbolises this.

The Empress (Mythic Tarot)

Other versions of this card convey the same ideas equally well, but use different imagery to do so. In the Mythic Tarot, for instance, The Empress is again portrayed as the goddess Demeter, holding ears of wheat and walking through a field in which red flowers grow. She wears a necklace of twelve stones symbolising the signs of the zodiac which relate to the cycle of the year with its changing seasons, important in cultivation. On her head is a crown in the form of a castle, reminding us, as in the Motherpeace image, that this card is not just about physical fertility, but also about civilised comforts, stable relationships and a secure home. A waterfall in the background signifies feeling and fertility, connected with the ideas of love, marriage and motherhood, also suggested by her pregnant appearance.

The Empress (Crowley Thoth Tarot)

In the Crowley Thoth deck, the card of The Empress depicts a woman seated in profile, holding a lotus flower over her breast. With her other arm she makes an embracing, protective gesture. The cup-shaped lotus is a feminine symbol; its form is supposed to be suggestive of female genitals, so it can be seen as representing sexuality and childbirth. Because the lotus is a water plant, its meaning is also related to the meanings associated with water, such as emotion, love, and the unconscious mind. It symbolises birth, evolution and spiritual wholeness.

The figure wears a horned crown reminiscent of that worn by the Egyptian goddess Hathor, who was often represented as a cow. This can remind us of the domestication of cattle, as the bull does in the Motherpeace image. Her belt is decorated with the signs of the zodiac, having the same significance as the necklace in the Mythic Tarot.

In the foreground is a pelican, nourishing its young with its own blood, symbolising the self-sacrificing love of idealised motherhood. At the top of the card are a sparrow and a dove, which are birds of Venus. The sparrow signifies sexual appetite; but we might also use this symbol to remind us of the comforts of home, since house sparrows live in the eaves of buildings and people often put out food and water for them. The dove stands for love, peace and fidelity.

The Thoth design is rather abstract, incorporating circular and crescent forms representing the moon — a feminine symbol. The softly curving shapes and pastel colouring of this card create a mood of peace and tranquillity, also related to the divinatory meaning. In the Thoth Tarot, the symbolic role of colour is particularly evident, but to some extent it may convey meaning in other decks as well, so this is a further aspect which can be considered when looking for meaning in the pictures.

The Empress (Barbara Walker Tarot)

In the Barbara Walker deck, we see many of the same symbols in the card of The Empress which we encountered in the other versions. The woman holds an ear of wheat and sits beside a waterfall — both the wheat and the waterfall being features which appear in the Mythic Tarot version already discussed, and which are also in the Rider-Waite version. In her book, *The Secrets of the Tarot* (pp. 70-71), Barbara Walker observes that the image of the wheat and the waterfall is a Gnostic earth-and-sea fertility symbol which has been adopted by the Freemasons.

In the bottom left corner of the card is a white lily, representing, like the lotus in Crowley's version, female genitals. Flying overhead is a dove — the bird of Venus already discussed. Above the figure of the Empress is a pennant bearing the head of a white horse, which is a symbol associated with goddess worship. The name of the Celtic goddess Epona means 'the big mare', and the word 'pony' is derived from it. Her attribute was a cornucopia — a symbol of abundance, as already explained — and her cult was probably associated with fertility.

The Empress (Medieval Scapini Tarot)

Lastly we shall examine the Medieval Scapini version of The Empress. Once again, some of the themes are familiar. Her dress is red for passion, and blue, representing water (fertility and emotion, as before). The lily is also present (though according to Scapini this stands for purity) and so is the crescent moon. The zodiac is represented as a crown of twelve stars (which also appears in the Rider-Waite version), but there are nine additional stars representing the muses of music, poetry and science. Furthermore, Scapini includes images representing the seven liberal arts, emphasising, as we have already mentioned, that artistic and spiritual qualities and the values of civilisation are important aspects of the card's meaning.

This brief survey of some of the designs for the card of The Empress should give an indication of how the symbolism in the picture relates to the divinatory meaning. Studying in this way the symbolism in the deck which you are using, so grasping the concepts around which the meaning is formed, can be an easier method of remembering the meanings of the cards than trying to memorise written phrases and sentences which you have read in a book.

It also seems wise to mention here briefly the matter of reverse meanings — that is, the meaning attributed to a card when it appears upside down in a spread. Reverse meanings are usually negative aspects of upright meanings, or an absence of qualities associated with the upright meaning. Although these may be a little more difficult to remember (since they are not directly related to the pictures on the cards), once an understanding of the upright meanings has been mastered, learning the reverse meanings can be fairly straightforward. However, we shall have more to say about the significance of reversed cards in Chapter 2, and since some Tarot readers prefer to interpret all the cards as if they are upright anyway, we do not need to say too much at this stage about reverse meanings. If you are a complete beginner to Tarot reading, you may prefer to disregard them until you become more experienced.

Telling a Story

Story-telling can be particularly helpful when you are learning the meanings of the numbered cards of the Minor Arcana. Fully pictorial decks have pictures on the Pip cards which, rather than being symbolic in the way that the Major Arcana images are, seem more like illustrations to a story. To help you to remember the meaning, try to see what is going on in the picture. Imagine what happened before the scene depicted, imagine what is going to happen afterwards, and make up a little story around it.

As an example, let us take the Ten of Wands. In the Hanson-Roberts deck, this card is called the Ten of Rods, and shows a man carrying a bundle of ten rods; in the distance is the castle which is his destination. By his posture we can judge that he is weighed down by a heavy burden. As he is an elderly man, this appears particularly difficult for him, and quite literally he has taken on more than he can handle.

Ten of Rods (Hanson-Roberts Tarot)

The meaning of this card is that one should beware of taking on too many responsibilities and trying to do too many things at once: a case of ambition causing someone to over-estimate his or her capacities. The Hanson-Roberts picture is a very apt image to illustrate the idea. If we imagine how the man got into this situation, we can understand more of the meaning. Perhaps not all the rods are his — as a favour, he may be carrying a friend's as well as his own. This relates to another aspect of the meaning — doing things which really ought to be the responsibility of others.

In the picture, the man's destination looks a long way off. If he continues struggling with this burden, it is clear that he will either collapse under the strain or be forced to drop some of his rods on the way (though he may come back later to pick them up). This is a metaphor for dealing with a few tasks at a time, giving up less important projects, perhaps with the idea of coming back to them later on when other work has been completed.

The upright meaning of the card concentrates on the more positive aspects — the desire to be active, busy and successful, and to help out others by taking on many commitments. The reverse meaning emphasises negative aspects — feeling exhausted, behaving incompetently, and not trusting other people to take responsibility for what needs to be done.

Other versions of this card bear a completely different image, and it may not be immediately clear how the picture connects to the meaning, so we shall examine three more versions in order to show that, despite the variations, the same ideas are usually represented.

Ten of Wands (Medieval Scapini Tarot)

In the Medieval Scapini deck, the Ten of Wands depicts two merchants leading heavily-laden mules along a road where ten armed bandits lie in wait for them, concealed behind trees and bushes. Although this is entirely different from the Hanson-Roberts version, we can see that the picture illustrates the same concepts. The merchants, in trying to transport all their wares at once, encounter problems which could have been avoided. The mules may collapse under the load even if the bandits do not ambush the party. Furthermore the bandits can see that these are successful and wealthy merchants, so they are a conspicuous target for attack, almost inviting trouble. Perhaps also the merchants are taking a short cut through the woods instead of using a safer route. The two merchants are no match for ten armed bandits, so if they attempt to defend themselves, again this would be taking on more than they can handle. In all, this is a very clear image of people who have over-estimated their capacities; their success, ambition and overconfidence have led them into a situation which they cannot cope with.

Ten of Wands (Mythic Tarot)

In the Mythic Tarot, the picture on the Ten of Wands is very different. It shows a king surrounded by ten flaming wands which make a kind of cage in which he is imprisoned. In the background is the wreck of a ship, in the foreground a fleece. This image represents the Greek hero Jason who, having successfully completed his quest for the Golden Fleece, became King of Iolkos. Unfortunately he did not know when enough was enough, and sought to become King of Corinth as well — a course of action which led to disaster and loss.

In the picture on the Tarot card, the Golden Fleece and Jason's ship, the Argo, lie abandoned, while the flaming wands, which represent his former success and ambition, have now become a cage in which he is trapped. As with the other versions of this card, we can see how this illustrates the idea of taking on too many responsibilities, over-estimating one's capacities and so encountering problems which would not have arisen if one had been less ambitious and had not tried to do too much at once.

In Barbara Walker's version of the Ten of Wands there is yet another image. A king watches as a second figure falls down into a

Ten of Wands (Barbara Walker Tarot)

dark and apparently bottomless void. The card is entitled Oppression (a title which also appears on the Crowley Thoth version of the Ten of Wands). In *The Secrets of the Tarot* (pp. 177-8), Barbara Walker explains that her picture for this card relates to the story of the Fall of Lucifer who challenged God's authority and was cast out of Heaven for the sin of pride, thus becoming Satan, the Devil.

As an illustration of the card's meaning, this image is interesting because it can be interpreted in two ways. According to the normal Christian tradition, Lucifer was over-ambitious in the extreme, endeavouring to do something which was far beyond his capacity. In this respect the card depicts a situation similar to that shown in the versions which we have already discussed. However, Walker portrays the king (who represents God) standing with his arms folded and with an expression of grim satisfaction on his face, as if he is gloating over the downfall of one who is weaker than himself. She explains that this is an allusion to the Gnostic belief that the universe is ruled by a malevolent deity and that Lucifer was right in opposing the tyrant's power. According to this view, it is the king in Walker's picture who has taken on too much by refusing to delegate authority, so becoming an oppressor. This emphasises another meaning which some commentators, including Waite and Crowley, have attributed to this card, concerning the dangerous, destructive and selfish traits which may be displayed by someone who has become extremely successful and who has too much power.

The Tarot deck which you are using may have an image on the Ten of Wands which differs from all four versions which we have described here, but we hope that, by following these examples, you get an idea of how to use the pictures on the Pip cards of the Minor Arcana to make up a story (or to remind you of an existing story) which relates to the meaning of each card.

Key Words

Another way of remembering the meanings is to choose a word or short phrase for each card which sums up an important aspect of the meaning. This is usually called a Key Word, and some decks have Key Words already printed on the cards — for example, the Barbara Walker and Crowley Thoth Tarots, as already mentioned. In this book we have provided, for each card, some Key Words which summarise the main points of the meaning. Sometimes, when appropriate, we have used the Golden Dawn's Key Words (which are also those used by Crowley and, to a lesser extent, Walker).

The Key Words can be used in two ways. Firstly, you can memorise a word for each card and then build the rest of the meaning around that word. The other way of using Key Words is to write the words you have chosen on the cards so that you do not have to memorise them, but can use them to remind you of the meanings.

You may be reluctant to write on your cards for fear of spoiling them, but there is no reason why words should deface the cards if they are written neatly. We have done this in the past, while learning the Tarot, and found it helpful, especially when using decks which had no pictures on the Pip cards. Also, in the case of the non-pictorial decks, some of the cards look the same when they are reversed as when they are upright, so, if reverse meanings are being used, it is necessary to indicate which is the top. A very fine permanent marker pen (of the sort used for overhead projectors) is best for writing on the glossy surface with which most cards are finished. Ball point ink looks messy and tends to rub off, but some semi-glossy surfaces will take Indian ink.

When using Key Words, it is important to recognise that they are only a starting point around which you can build up the rest of the meaning. They are not a substitute for applying more detailed meanings, and they should not make you feel constrained to keep to some narrow interpretation suggested by the Key Word. Key Words are only an aid to the memory — not an excuse for doing crude and inaccurate readings.

Personal Experience

Finally, personal experience is one of the most important ways of learning Tarot meanings.

As you think about the meaning of each card, try to relate it to a personal experience; this will not only help you to remember it, but will probably give you greater insight into the card's meaning, as it will not then simply be something you read in a book but something which has personal significance for you.

When studying the Court cards, it is particularly useful to associate each card with a friend or relative. You can start by finding the Court card which most accurately fits your own personality, or a predominant aspect of your personality. Then you can choose cards to represent your mother, your father, and other members of your family; or you can read each of the Court card meanings and consider whether you have ever met anyone like that. You may wish to see the reverse aspects of these cards as distinct personalities; on the other hand, they could be the negative traits of the personalities represented by the upright meanings.

The Court cards tend to have rather extreme character traits and are perhaps more like caricatures than real people, who have more subtle personalities. Nevertheless, it should be possible to make associations between at least some of the Court cards and real people you have met. For the rest, you may like to use fictional characters from your favourite novels or television programmes. Describing the personality of a friend, relative or familiar fictional character which you associate with a particular Court card is much easier than trying to memorise the meaning for that card which you have read in a book.

Personal experience is also very important in a more general sense when learning how to do Tarot readings. One of the best ways to learn how to do readings is actually to do them; there is only a certain amount of preparation which can be made in advance. Studying the cards in the context of a spread, and attaching the meanings to real situations in the life of the person for whom you are doing the reading, is ultimately the most effective way of mastering the Tarot.

CHAPTER TWO

DOING A READING

Ritual procedures

When using Tarot cards for divination it has become customary to observe various ritual practices, which apply not only during the course of a reading, but also to the storing and handling of the cards. These can range from formal ceremonies in which ritual objects are used and spiritual forces invoked, to simply performing the reading in a pleasant environment and adopting a suitably calm frame of mind. Although elaborate procedures are not strictly necessary, and most Tarot readings are done without the assistance of spirits, some sort of formal approach is probably more conducive to doing better readings.

There are two main reasons for this. One is that a Tarot card reading is a means of bringing into consciousness intuitive feelings and unconscious impressions, tapping that part of the mind which is not restricted by an ordinary awareness of time and which can therefore sometimes disclose helpful advice about the future. In order to become aware of unconscious impressions, it is necessary to quieten the conscious mind. If either the Tarot reader or the person for whom the reading is done (called the Querent) is in an excited, nervous or emotionally disturbed state, it is difficult to get a clear and coherent reading. Small rituals, such as lighting incense or saying a prayer, and also procedures involving shuffling and counting out the cards according to a predetermined routine, can be a way of calming the mind and creating the right atmosphere.

A second way in which observing certain rituals can be helpful is in forming a fixed framework within which apparently chance or random elements involved in divination can operate. Tarot reading, like many forms of divination, employs chance, in that the cards are shuffled and selected at random. In order to make sense out of any random features in divination, to see a meaningful pattern within what is superficially random and meaningless, it is necessary to make a sharp distinction between the factors of the situation which are supposed to be random, where chance or fate operates, and those which are fixed and constant. The concepts of chance and randomness make sense only against an orderly and fixed background, and this would be lost if the whole proceedings were chaotic and disorderly. So for this reason also it is a good idea to follow some ritual, if only in the shuffling and selection of the cards.

Traditionally, Tarot cards are wrapped up in black silk and stored in a wooden box. The silk and wood are said to be good psychic insulators, keeping the cards free from external influences. As we have already mentioned, you should use your own cards and not those belonging to someone else. Wrapping them in silk is a further way of making them personal to you, keeping them free of psychic contamination. For the same reason you should not allow other people to play with your cards or handle them, except in the context of a reading when the Querent shuffles them and makes a selection.

When laying out the cards in a spread, it is also a good idea to lay them on a cloth used specially for this purpose. It is traditional for this cloth, like the wrapper, to be made of black silk, but a large piece of heavy black silk is expensive, so you may want to use a different material, though black is still the best colour.

Ideally you should make the box, wrapper and tablecloth yourself, but you will probably not be inclined to do this unless you have the required skills. Nevertheless, you can personalise these items by putting your own decorations on a box or tablecloth which you have bought or which someone else has made for you; while the cards can be imbued with your own psychic vibrations by carrying them in your pocket or sleeping with them under the pillow when you first acquire them.

Try to avoid doing a reading in a situation where there is a group of onlookers talking, sniggering, smoking and drinking, making rude remarks or causing other distractions. Even the presence of one person behaving in this way can make a Tarot reading into a farce. This may sound obvious, but you may be surprised how often you are asked to read the cards in such circumstances — at a party, for instance, or with a group of friends — and on the spur of the moment it can be difficult to refuse without disappointing people.

The best readings are obtained when you are alone with the Querent in a quiet room. Take a few minutes to relax before starting the reading, and perform whatever ritual practices seem to you to create a pleasant and appropriate atmosphere, such as burning incense or lighting candles. If you like, you can say a short prayer. Here is one that was used by the Golden Dawn:

In the divine name IAO, I invoke Thee thou Great Angel HRU who art set over the operations of this Secret Wisdom. Lay thine hand invisibly on these consecrated cards of art, that thereby I may obtain knowledge of hidden things, to the glory of the ineffable Name. Amen.

(An Introduction to the Golden Dawn Tarot, page 104)

The Querent should be asked to think about the matter on which guidance is sought. Writing down a question which he or she would like answered is a way to help focus the concentration. It is not necessary for the Querent to tell you, the reader, what the question is, but it may be useful for you to know the sort of question being asked — for instance, if it requires a specific yes or no answer, or whether a decision is to be made between various alternative courses of action — in order that you be able to choose an appropriate spread. Some spreads are more suitable for answering one sort of question than another.

Selecting the cards for a spread

Before you start to shuffle the cards, decide on the spread which you are going to use. (A variety of spreads is provided at the end of this chapter.)

Some books on the Tarot recommend choosing a Significator. This is a card which represents the Querent, or sometimes the situation about which advice is being sought. If it is to represent the Querent, this card is usually a Court card and is chosen on the basis of the Querent's hair or eye colouring, or astrological sign. (We say more about this at the beginning of Chapter 5.) A card to represent a situation could be any card whose meaning aptly describes that situation. If a Significator is being used, it should be removed from the deck before shuffling and placed face up on the table as a focus for the Tarot reader's concentration. However, we do not use a Significator because we have found it unnecessary, and it also has the disadvantage of removing one card from the deck which could have provided more helpful information if it had been allowed to come up in the spread in the natural course of a reading.

The cards should be well shuffled before each reading. If you are going to use reverse meanings, you need to ensure that roughly half the cards in the deck are reversed, so turn some round as you shuffle them, and make sure that they are well mixed in among the others. Also if you are using reverse meanings it is important that the cards are kept in the correct orientation as they are passed between Querent and reader. This means that you must not reverse the whole pack when handing the cards to the Querent or after they have been handed back to you, or the reading will be upside down.

When you have shuffled the cards, hand them to the Querent to shuffle. When the Querent hands them back, be careful not to turn them round. If the cards are handed back sideways, ask the Querent which end is to be the top, and turn the deck the right way round accordingly.

There are two ways in which the cards are commonly selected. One is to ask the Querent, using the left hand, to cut the deck twice — the first time to make a second pile to the left of the remaining cards in the first pile, and then again to make a third pile to the left of the second one. The three piles are then put together again so that the cards which were previously at the bottom are now on top. The Tarot reader then deals the appropriate number of cards off the top of the deck and lays them out in the positions for the chosen spread.

The second method of selection is to fan out the entire deck, face down, across the table and ask the Querent to pick the number of cards required from anywhere in the deck, being careful to keep them in the order they were chosen. This second method has the advantage of allowing greater choice to the Querent, but can sometimes lead to problems when a nervous Querent muddles the order of the cards or drops them on the floor. If this should happen, ask the Querent to pick up the cards and put them in any order of their own choice, but you must be sure that you know whether the first card of the sequence is on the top or the bottom of the pile, so that you can place the cards in the right positions in the spread. Some people, when choosing the cards, will put them one on top of another, so the first is at the bottom; while other people will put each card underneath the previously-chosen one. It is important to observe this, as well as take note of which way up the cards are supposed to be, so that they are laid out in the correct sequence and also are not inadvertently reversed.

Laying out and interpreting a spread

When you lay out the cards in a spread, place them face down, the first one chosen in position one, the second in position two, and so on. When they are correctly laid out, you can turn them face up, being careful to turn them over from side to side and not from end to end, which would reverse them.

When interpreting the spread, cards are to be regarded as upright or reversed from the point of view of the reader. (If the Querent is seated on the opposite side of the table, the spread is seen upside down from their point of view.) If you are not using reverse meanings, obviously you should turn any cards upright if they become accidentally reversed.

The practice of ascribing a different meaning to a card when it is reversed is fairly recent in the history of Tarot reading, and there is more disagreement about the meanings of reversed cards than about the meanings of the cards when they are upright. Some commentators say that the reverse meaning of a card should be the opposite of the upright meaning, so if an upright meaning is unpleasant, the reverse meaning of that card would be more favourable. However, we take the view that pictures are meant to be seen upright and that there seems to be something inherently unfavourable about an image appearing upside down. For this reason the reverse meanings that appear in this book are generally negative: they indicate impediments to attaining the positive qualities and conditions associated with a card's upright meaning, or, if the upright meaning already has unpleasant aspects, a worsening of that situation.

When you begin a reading, look at all the cards in the spread before starting to interpret them individually, so as to gain a general impression. See if there is a predominance of cards of any particular sort, or whether many are reversed, indicating obstacles and problems. If many of the cards belong to the Major Arcana, this is a sign that at this time there are forces for change in the Querent's life which are largely beyond their control but which will shape their destiny in important ways. A predominance of Court cards shows a strong influence from other people upon the Querent. If cards from any one suit of the Minor Arcana predominate, this suggests that the particular attributes of that suit are important in the Querent's life at this time; for instance, the presence of many cards from the suit of Wands may indicate that the Querent is interested in career prospects, or involved in enterprising projects, while a majority of

Cups would probably suggest that they are chiefly preoccupied with personal relationships and emotional matters. Swords indicate struggle, worry and conflict, while Coins show that practical affairs, money and security are the Querent's main concerns.

Try to get an impression of the general atmosphere of the spread, seeing it as a whole, rather than as being composed of separate cards. During the reading you should relate the cards together as much as possible, comparing and contrasting them, showing, for instance, how past events and influences connect to the present and to the future, and whether circumstances are changing for better or for worse. In certain spreads, the meaning of the cards is modified by the meaning of adjacent cards — especially in spreads where there is more than one card for each position. For example, if you were using a spread in which three cards were placed in a position which means 'chosen course of action', the cards would have to be interpreted in relation to one another to give a coherent picture of the course of action which the Querent has chosen.

Connecting the cards together in this way can be difficult for a beginner, when there are so many other factors which have to be taken into account at the same time. It may be helpful to sum up your remarks at the end of the reading, showing at this point how the cards interrelate, if you were not able to make this very clear at first. Summing up in this way not only helps the Querent to have a clearer idea of the main points in the reading, but will also help you to remember the meanings of the cards and to practise making connections between them, which will make this easier the next time you do a reading.

Some spreads to use

Most Tarot readers use a formal spread when interpreting the cards; that is, the cards are laid in a special pattern where each position has a particular meaning. It is not absolutely necessary to use a spread — some experienced readers prefer a more intuitive and open-ended approach, especially if clairvoyance is used — but a spread can help in making a reading more accurate by providing a framework within which each of the cards can be interpreted in relation to a specific area of the Querent's life. A spread, for instance, shows which cards say something about the Querent's past, and which relate to the future, which cards show the Querent's feelings and which show the feelings of other people, such as friends and relatives.

When interpreting the cards, you should adapt the general meaning of each card to make it appropriate to the position in which it appears in the spread. The position of a card in the spread can also help you to decide which aspects of the card's meaning are likely to apply in that particular reading. For example, the card of The Emperor can mean that the Querent is going to be promoted at work; however, if this card appears in a position called Home Life, it is less likely to have this meaning, since the position is supposed to reveal matters concerning the Querent's personal affairs rather than what is happening at work. In this case, the card of The Emperor is more likely to indicate that the Querent has a responsible position at home, is regarded as head of the household, expected to make the important decisions for the rest of the family, and so on.

In this section we show you three spreads, each of which is suitable for answering a particular sort of question. In the final section of this chapter are two more spreads, demonstrated by means of sample readings.

In a complete reading, it is normal to use two or three spreads, starting with one of a simple or general nature, to gain an overview of the Querent's situation, but leaving spreads which answer a specific question (such as the Alternatives Spread, or the Yes or No Spread) until the end. The interpretation of a spread should take about ten or fifteen minutes, depending upon its complexity, so the reading as a whole should take between half and three-quarters of an hour. It is inadvisable to spend more than an hour on a reading, as this is not only exhausting for the reader, but confusing for the Querent too, who will probably forget much of what has been said.

DOING A READING

Seven Card Horseshoe Spread

This spread is suitable for giving guidance on a specific problem, when the Querent is unsure about what to do for the best.

After shuffling and selection of the cards, as described above, the chosen cards are laid out according to the diagram.

The first card reveals something about the Querent's past. This is not some vague or general notion of the past, however, but something specific which relates to the present problem about which the Querent is seeking advice. It may show events leading up to the present situation. On the other hand, it may allude to a similar situation in the past, reminding the Querent of how they coped then. Perhaps there is no direct connection between this past situation and the present problem, but the card could be telling the Querent to make use of past experience, either to avoid repeating mistakes, or to employ tactics which previously proved to be effective.

Card number 2 shows the present, and may elucidate the problem which the Querent is concerned about. This card should be compared and contrasted with the cards in both position 1 and position 3 (which represents the future) to see whether circumstances will improve or deteriorate.

You may be wondering what is the difference between position 3, showing the future, and 7, showing the outcome. Many spreads have a position called Outcome, as well as one called Future, but they do not necessarily mean the same. The Outcome card may, for example, show the course of action which the Querent is most likely to take, while the card in position 3 shows the result of this in the future. On the other hand, the Outcome card often sums up the Querent's feelings about the whole situation — particularly feelings experienced when looking back on this situation, after it is all over. This is not the same as a future event, though it may represent a future mental or emotional state of the Querent.

Card number 4 indicates the best course of action to resolve the problem on which guidance is sought. This card should be compared with those in positions 3 and 7, to see whether the Querent is going to follow this advice or not. Though agreeing that

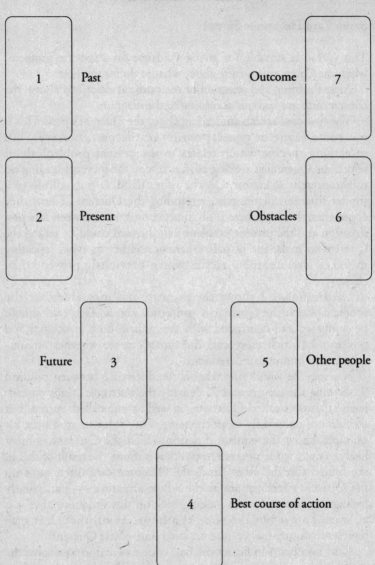

Seven Card Horseshoe Spread

it is the best thing to do, the Querent may still prefer to act otherwise, and it could be enlightening to explore the reasons for this.

The card in position 5 shows how other people feature in the Querent's problem. It may indicate how others around the Querent are behaving, or how they feel about what is happening. Of course, it may be the behaviour of other people which is causing the present problem, and this card may reveal something helpful about their role in the situation. On the other hand, the card in this position could show who is supportive and sympathetic to the Querent's point of view.

The card in position 6 reveals any obstacles to resolving the problem. It may, for example, show why (if this is indeed the case) the Querent is not going to take the best course of action but do something else instead. The obstacles could be something of which the Querent is already aware, but alternatively this card could warn the Querent of a danger which they have not anticipated. If the card has a favourable meaning, this may pose problems of interpretation, because although it could be a sign that the Querent faces no obstacles, there are other possible interpretations. For example, certain attitudes or situations may be generally considered good, but they could still be inappropriate in certain contexts. Even feeling happy and contented could be an obstacle in some circumstances if it made the Querent avoid taking a course of action which is necessary in order to achieve a desired result.

As with any spread, the numbers of the positions indicate the order in which the cards are to be laid out, and not necessarily the order in which to interpret them. You can talk about the cards in any order which seems most meaningful to you, and relate them together in any way which seems helpful.

Golden Dawn Spread

This spread is based on one which was used by the Order of the Golden Dawn. It is a fairly thorough spread, revealing much about the Querent's situation and feelings, and giving advice about which course of action to take in a situation where various options are

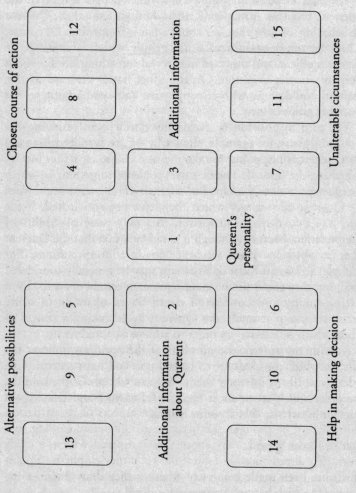

Chosen course of action

Additional information

Unalterable circumstances

Querent's personality

Golden Dawn Spread

Alternative possibilities

Additional information about Querent

Help in making decision

12	8	4
15	11	3
		7
	1	
5	2	6
9		10
13		14

possible and it is hard to decide what to do. Unlike some spreads, which seem to show a fixed, determined future (worrying some people who think this means that their experiences are fated to happen, no matter what they themselves decide to do), this one makes it clear that how the Querent acts is a matter of personal choice.

You will notice that there are three cards for each position, so it is particularly important to interpret the cards in relation to one another.

Cards 1, 2 and 3 provide information about the Querent. The first card indicates the Querent's personality or feelings at this time, while the other two cards may elaborate upon this, or reveal something about the present situation or the problem on which the Querent is seeking guidance.

Cards 4, 8 and 12 show what will happen if the Querent continues on course, doing what he or she feels most inclined to do at the moment. Each of the three cards in this position may show a different aspect of the situation which will come about, or they may show a sequence of events. It is up to you to decide which is the most appropriate interpretation.

Cards 5, 9 and 13 indicate alternative courses of action — what the Querent can do if deciding against the option shown in 4, 8 and 12. Again, you can see each of the three cards as representing distinct events or actions, or see them as various aspects of one course of action. Cards 4, 8 and 12 should be compared with 5, 9 and 13 to see whether the course of action which the Querent is contemplating is the wisest thing to do, or whether there is a better alternative.

Cards 6, 10 and 14 show factors which are helpful in making the decision about what to do. They may represent people who could help the Querent, or they may indicate aspects of the situation which should be thought about very carefully before coming to a final decision. Again, they should be compared with the cards which have already been interpreted to see if they emphasise a point which has been made before, or whether they draw attention to something which has not yet been considered.

Sometimes there is difficulty in interpreting cards in a position called Help, if they seem to suggest something unpleasant, in the same way that cards with a pleasant meaning can be difficult to interpret in a position of Obstacles. If the cards in the Help position seem unfavourable, this may mean that the Querent is unlikely to receive help. However, they could still signify factors which need to be taken into account when making a decision, and in this way may be regarded as helpful. It is also worth considering, when interpreting the cards in this position, that apparent misfortunes can sometimes have positive features to them or be blessings in disguise.

Finally, cards 7, 11 and 15 show the circumstances which are beyond the control of the Querent. These are features of the situation which cannot be changed by any action of the Querent but which are still important and have to be taken into account when deciding what to do. Even though the Querent cannot change these circumstances, he or she may be able to adapt to them, so as to make the best of an existing situation.

Yes or No Spread

As the title suggests, this spread can be used when a question requires a 'yes' or 'no' answer. Before selection of the cards, the deck should be shuffled so that some of the cards are reversed. If four or more are upright when the cards are laid out, the answer is probably 'yes', and if four or more are reversed, the answer is probably 'no'. However, the meanings of the cards also have to be taken into account, because sometimes four upright cards may still suggest a negative answer if the meanings of the cards seem very unfavourable to the outcome which the Querent desires. The more upright cards there are, the more strongly a 'yes' answer is indicated, and likewise, a large number of reversed cards strongly suggests 'no'.

However, care should also be taken about the wording of the question when using this spread. Try to avoid questions which are phrased in a negative way, because this can make the answer ambiguous. For example, do not ask a question like 'Will I fail the exam?' or 'Is my husband being unfaithful?' How could you possibly interpret the answer? If the cards were upright and the meanings were favourable to the Querent, would this mean 'Yes,

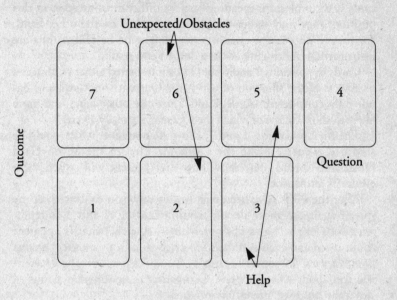

Yes or No Spread

you will fail,' and 'Yes, your husband is unfaithful'? Presumably the Querent wants to pass the exam, so upright cards with a favourable meaning ought to indicate that they will pass, but the negative form of the question suggests otherwise.

To avoid this confusion, the question should be worded so that a 'yes' answer corresponds to the situation which the Querent desires, and a 'no' answer corresponds to what they hope will not come about. Also it should be recognised that a 'no' answer does not mean 'never', but only indicates that what the Querent desires will not happen in the near future.

The card in position number 4 indicates what the question is about, showing the Querent's chief concerns at this time.

Cards 3 and 5 show features of the situation which are helpful to the Querent. As we saw in the previous spread, reversed cards or cards with unpleasant meanings can be difficult to interpret in this position: they may indicate a lack of help, but on the other hand, apparently unpleasant circumstances might be helpful if they are instrumental in bringing about a desired end result.

Cards in positions 2 and 6 should be interpreted either as obstacles or aspects of the situation of which the Querent is not aware or has not fully considered. Cards 3 and 5, on the other hand, are more likely to show factors of which the Querent is already aware.

The final two cards, 1 and 7, show the outcome, which could be a future event, or, like the Outcome card in the Seven Card Horseshoe Spread, may show how the Querent will regard these events in retrospect.

After the cards have been read in this way, you can interpret the spread again, in more depth, treating cards 1, 2 and 3 as representations of the Querent's outer life — that is, what is apparent about them and events in their life when seen from another person's point of view. In contrast, cards 5, 6 and 7 show how the Querent will feel about what happens. Comparing these different points of view may produce interesting insights.

You will see from the descriptions of these spreads that there is no definite or correct way of doing a Tarot reading, for much depends upon an individual reader's own style and approach. Each reading you do will be different, so a way of interpreting the cards on one occasion may be inappropriate on another. The meaning of each position in a spread, like the meaning attached to each of the cards, is only a guide for interpretation, and can be adapted as appropriate. As you develop your skill in Tarot reading, you will acquire an increasingly creative and intuitive approach, and will find your own ways of using the spreads, or even make up new ones to suit particular needs.

Celtic Cross Spread: A Sample Reading

The Celtic Cross is one of the most popular spreads, and it appears in many books on the Tarot. There are several variations of it, though they are essentially similar.

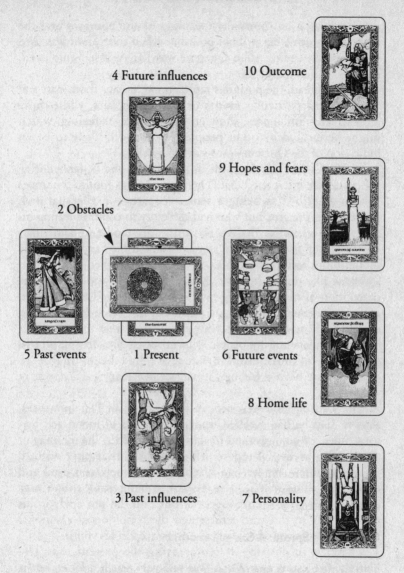

4 Future influences

10 Outcome

9 Hopes and fears

2 Obstacles

5 Past events

1 Present

6 Future events

8 Home life

3 Past influences

7 Personality

Celtic Cross Spread
illustrated with the Norse Tarot

The illustration shows the meanings of the positions and the cards which came up in those positions when this spread was used in an actual reading. The Querent was Mr A, a self-employed, married man in his forties.

In this spread, the positions representing 'events' (both past and future) show particular events or states of affairs, while those representing 'influences' show an atmosphere or feeling, which might be created by other people, but is more likely to be an indication of the Querent's own state of mind.

In Mr A's reading, the cards in positions 3 and 5, representing the past, were interpreted first. The King of Cups (position number 5) was described as being a sensitive, rather intellectual man interested in the arts, but who had difficulty in communicating his feelings to others, so that he was misunderstood and sometimes mistrusted by those who did not understand him and mistakenly thought him to be cool and aloof. When asked whether there was someone like this in his past, Mr A said that it was an accurate description of himself during his teens, twenties and early thirties. He was a talented musician and artist, but had been unable to find an outlet for developing his creative abilities at that time, and had been misunderstood by people who expected him to conform to their idea of normality. Because he had been unable to communicate his real feelings, it had seemed that he did not fit in with others.

The Two of Coins reversed, in the position of Past Influences, showed that he had suffered from fluctuations of mood and had sometimes felt confused and unable to cope. When the meaning of the card was explained to him, he said that this was an understatement, for he had often felt extremely confused and depressed. The manic, irresponsible behaviour sometimes associated with the reverse aspect of this card did not apply in his case: for Mr A, this card represented the condition of emotional turmoil and distress which he had experienced in his youth.

The card in position 1, representing the present, was The Hermit, suggesting that Mr A was still very much a loner, but it seemed that his attitude to this had now changed. The Hermit indicated that he felt independent and enjoyed doing things by himself, in his own way, and that he no longer experienced distress and confusion about not conforming to other people's expectations. He agreed with this, for he had now become self-employed, and regularly performed as a professional musician.

The card in position 2, representing obstacles to the Querent's desires and goals is laid across the first card, but should be interpreted as if it were upright. This may sound strange, as it could seem hard to interpret as an obstacle a card in this position with a pleasant meaning. In practice, however, it is usually possible to find a suitable interpretation. In Mr A's reading, the card in this position was the Ace of Coins, suggesting that Mr A had a problem regarding money and security, and also that he may have a problem about enjoying the pleasures of the senses, relaxing and having a good time. This was indeed the case, for he was suffering the experience of many self-employed people, finding himself working long hours to make more money for his small business, though this left him very little time for relaxation. Despite this, he had financial difficulties and said that it seemed there were not enough hours in the day to do the work to make the money that he and his family needed. 'I'd like to think we can have a bit more freedom not to be so tied to making money — more time to spend it and enjoy it,' he explained.

The card in position 6, representing future events, was the Ten of Cups reversed. This indicated that in the future Mr A would still be having problems in his relationships with other people. He was told that the reverse meaning of this card suggested that he would be in a group of people, one of whom would feel dissatisfied with a situation that was enjoyed by all the others. When asked if this meant anything to him, and whether he thought such a future event likely or knew who the dissatisfied person might be, he replied that he had often had such an experience before. For instance, he disliked working with others. 'They don't pay attention to detail,' he said, 'which I do — but then, they probably think I'm being too fussy. Usually the person who's dissatisfied is me,' he added with an ironic laugh.

The card of The Sun in position 4 indicated that future influences were very favourable. In contrast with the card representing past influences (which showed Mr A being confused and depressed), The Sun suggested that in the future he would feel optimistic and enthusiastic, that he would have realistic ambitions and high ideals, and that he would strive to fulfil himself.

Interpreted in combination with the Ten of Cups reversed in position 6, and compared with the cards representing the past and the present, this seemed to show that the main changes which had taken place were in Mr A's self-esteem. In the past, he had felt bad about being an individualist and was confused about his own desires and goals because he could not make himself understood. At present he feels much more confident about being independent, is successfully working on his own, and developing his creative talents. The cards for the future indicate that he will still have problems about working with others and in compromising his own desires and standards to conform to what others want, but this will no longer worry him because he will have much more faith in his own convictions, and will enjoy the confidence and the opportunities to pursue his ambitions.

The card in position 7 was the Four of Wands reversed, and this revealed some different aspects of Mr A's personality which had not been apparent in the reading until this point. The reader first interpreted this card to mean that Mr A felt restricted and inhibited by outside constraints put upon him, and by rules and regulations imposed by others. This is the traditional meaning of the reverse aspect of the Four of Wands, and seemed consistent with the interpretation of previous cards in the spread. However, Mr A disagreed with this, saying that there was a sense in which he liked rules and regulations. Although when he was younger he had sometimes seemed to be a misfit, he had never been wild or rebellious. 'I never liked going out on a limb,' he said. 'I'm happy to work within an accepted framework, but just like putting my own influence on things. I like things to be regulated, and I like to create within a framework, otherwise, to me, it ceases to be art or music and becomes just noise or splodges. Creativity is an ordered form of things — not disorder.'

Thus, the idea of restrictions and regulations imposed upon creativity and self-expression — which for many people is a negative meaning of the Four of Wands — had positive connotations for Mr A, because he interpreted this as referring to self-imposed regulations and a form of personal discipline which he valued. This orderliness was in fact a crucial feature of his personality, and one which (according to his comments on the interpretation of the Ten of Cups reversed) was often seen by others as fussiness.

The King of Swords reversed in position 8, representing the Querent's home life, posed certain problems in interpretation often encountered with Court cards. Because of the negative associations of the reverse aspect of this card, it was at first suggested that an unpleasant man was upsetting Mr A's private life, but this interpretation was wrong.

Another meaning of this card concerns injustice, a sense of unfairness, and an inappropriate use of the intellect. When Mr A was asked if he felt that someone at home was treating him unfairly, he said that he sometimes felt picked on. He spoke cautiously about this, saying he felt that it was 'a bit unfair', and that 'someone has a short fuse', but he attributed this person's shortness of temper to tiredness and worry, and made allowances for them. It seemed that he was talking about his wife, but when the point was pursued further, it turned out that Mr A himself was manifesting some of the attributes of the King of Swords reversed. He confessed that it was he, and not his wife, who was sometimes behaving in an inappropriately cool and rational way, trying to deal with emotional problems on an intellectual level.

The Queen of Wands in position 9 was also puzzling to interpret at first, as it is hard to understand how the personality represented by a Court card could be a hope or a fear (the meaning of a card in this position). The Queen of Wands was described to Mr A as being someone who was lively, sociable, possessing diverse skills in both business and home-making, and also having warm and passionate qualities. It was suggested to him that possibly he wanted to be like this himself, or that he would like his wife to be like this, or that he would like to meet someone with these characteristics. Mr A assented to all these interpretations, saying that he wanted to experience in some way the qualities described, but that it did not especially matter to him whether he found them in himself or in someone else. They seemed to be qualities which were lacking in his life at present, and for which he felt a need.

Reflecting on both the King of Swords reversed and the Queen of Wands, he said that he felt that most problems were of an intellectual nature and were to be dealt with rationally. Then he had a sudden flash of insight. 'I suppose that could be a protective strategy,' he admitted. 'On an intellectual level, I'm not vulnerable, because you can always find out about what you don't know. There's no competition because, to get the knowledge you need, you can go somewhere or ask someone else. But on an emotional level, something always happens where you get hurt in the end. If I didn't mind being hurt, perhaps I could get what I want emotionally, and begin to experience deeper emotions.'

This deeper level of emotional experience was represented by the Queen of Wands in the position of Hopes and Fears, and, in the light of Mr A's remarks, it appeared that the card could be interpreted as both a hope and a fear: he wanted to experience the passion, energy and enthusiasm of the Queen of Wands, but at the same time was afraid of being hurt by engaging with people on an emotional level. These ideas were discussed further, in relation to Mr A's personality in the past, as represented by the King of Cups.

The final card, the Two of Wands, showed how Mr A would view this period of his life in retrospect. It indicated that he would see this as a time in which he overcame former obstacles and established a firm foundation upon which to build future success. It showed that he had achieved much already, which would have seemed impossible at the time when he was confused and depressed, but this card can also indicate that the Querent is not fully able to enjoy or appreciate personal achievement which is experienced to some extent as an anti-climax. This seemed to be true of Mr A, in that he was worried by financial problems and lack of leisure time (represented by the Ace of Coins in the position of Obstacles) which made it hard for him to recognise the positive aspects of his present situation.

The Two of Wands can often indicate that the Querent is having to reassess the situation and to make plans for the direction his or her career should take. At the time of the reading, Mr A was not aware of this, but some weeks later he was asked how he now felt about the reading. He said that he had been surprised by its accuracy and had found it to be helpful. In the days afterwards he had remembered what had been said and had seen further significance in it. He now realised that he was approaching a point in which he had to make an important decision about the way in which to develop his business. In retrospect, the traditional meaning of the Two of Wands turned out to be a very appropriate description of Mr A's experience at the time of the reading.

Alternatives Spread: A Sample Reading

This spread is suitable for answering questions which take the form 'Should I...?' The Querent may ask a question in this form when he or she has in mind a particular course of action, but is unsure whether or not it is prudent and are wondering if an alternative course of action would be preferable.

The illustration shows the meanings of the positions and the cards which came up in those positions when this spread was used in an actual reading. The Querent was Mrs B — an attractive, divorced woman in her fifties, who worked as a secretary in a large comprehensive school. Mrs B's question was 'Should I remain in my present job?' It should be noted that the question took this form as opposed to 'Should I change my job?' This is because remaining in her present job was what she was most inclined to do and what, for the purpose of this spread, we shall call her 'chosen course of action'. You will see from the diagram that the cards in the top three positions (5, 1 and 3) represent what will happen if the Querent pursues their chosen course of action, and the bottom three cards (in positions 4, 2 and 6) represent what will happen if they pursue alternative possibilities.

The card in position 7 represents the fundamental nature of the Querent's problem. As with the 'Outcome' position in the Celtic Cross Spread, the card in this position may indicate how the Querent will view the situation when looking back on it afterwards.

In Mrs B's reading, the card in position 7 was the Six of Coins

Chosen course of action

1

5

3

7 Problem/Outcome

4

6

2

Alternative possibilities

Alternatives Spread
illustrated with the Norse Tarot

reversed, showing that what most concerned her was that in her present job she was contributing a great deal of work and effort, but not getting the recompense which she felt she deserved. She said that this interpretation was absolutely right. Her work was poorly paid and was, to some extent, unrewarding in other ways, as became apparent during the rest of the reading.

The cards in positions 5, 1 and 3 showed her experience of her job as a school secretary. The Ace of Cups reversed in position 5 indicated that her relationships with people at work were inadequate in some way: that there was a lack of friendship, care and emotional support. Mrs B agreed with this. 'On the whole,' she said, 'they're not entirely my sort of people. I suppose you get the feeling you're on your own in a place like that.' This seemed to be one of the main reasons for her discontent with the job, and not because the work in itself was boring.

This question of whether the work was boring arose when the card in position 3 was interpreted. The Page of Coins reversed can sometimes indicate that the Querent is engaged in a boring activity, but this was not true in Mrs B's case, so she disagreed with this interpretation. Instead, the card showed that she had to deal with petty-minded and pompous people who liked to exert their authority, and that this was very irritating and frustrating. She said that she was annoyed when some of the teaching staff behaved in this way. School life, she said, was really very petty when compared with the outside world, and she felt that some of the teachers had strange foibles and a very narrow view of life.

The King of Cups in position 1 at first seemed to represent the new headmistress, even though the Kings usually represent men. The headmaster had recently retired, and the new headmistress had been at the school for only a few weeks. The King of Cups is a cultured, intellectual person whose real personality is difficult to understand because he conceals his feelings. When Mrs B was asked if the headmistress was like this, she confessed her uneasiness: 'She seems quite friendly, but we're not sure if that's a front — whether she's being condescending to her office staff. Perhaps because it's all such early days, we're not going to get the full measure of her yet. She'll be making changes we don't yet know about.' It became apparent that the change of head was another reason why Mrs B had been feeling dissatisfied with her job. She had grown used to the headmaster and was finding it hard to adapt to working with the new headmistress — not because they had specific disagreements, but because Mrs B was uncomfortable about developing a working relationship with her.

Taking the three cards (5, 1 and 3) together, it was clear that the main problem with Mrs B's job was that she was not altogether happy with her colleagues and sometimes felt that she did not fit in. She perceived other members of staff as petty and 'living in their own little world', as she put it. This showed that in some respects the King of Cups could be seen as representing Mrs B herself, who was somewhat aloof in her relationships with colleagues, concealed her real feelings and felt herself to be intellectually superior to some of the people she encountered at work.

The cards in positions 4, 2 and 6 represented what Mrs B would experience if she were to seek other employment. The Nine of Wands indicated that she would find it hard to establish herself in a new job; that she would experience it as a struggle which required constant effort and battling against obstacles. Perhaps even finding a suitable job would be difficult. Mrs B agreed with this and said that she thought she would be silly to put herself in a such a position.

Temperance in position 2 indicated that a different job could offer Mrs B an opportunity to develop other abilities from those which she was using at present, and to express other aspects of her personality, providing her with more all-round satisfaction. She may also be able to develop more harmonious relationships with colleagues in a new job.

Mrs B felt that this was true, and it was this thought which had led her to wonder whether or not to stay in her present job, because she hoped that she may be able to find a more satisfying occupation. 'You'd get in with what I call normal people,' she remarked. 'School is really quite a strange environment.' However, her ideas about alternative work were rather vague and general, and she did not have a clear notion of what she would like to do. 'If I haven't changed my job, I'm not going to know if I'm going to get all-round satisfaction,' she said. 'I can't say the school job *isn't* satisfying.' Despite the problems in her present job, she was not sufficiently confident that she would benefit from changing it, and was inclined to avoid the effort and struggle which would be involved in making the attempt (as indicated by the Nine of Wands).

The Nine of Coins reversed in position 6 referred to the way in which her security would be undermined if she tried to start a new career so late in life. It will be noticed that there are three reversed Coin cards in the spread, emphasising Mrs B's concern with financial problems and lack of security. After the breakdown of her marriage, she had been obliged to return to full-time work, but few opportunities had been available to her. She was concerned about her low income and lack of provision for a pension, which contributed to a feeling of insecurity. The Nine of Coins reversed showed that to change her job would risk sacrificing the security which she already had, even though this was not altogether adequate. 'At my age,' she said, 'if I was to change, in no time at all I could be made redundant. I've got security at school until I retire.'

Overall, the reading confirmed that Mrs B was right in thinking that there would be no great advantage in changing her job. 'I don't think it would be practical to change at my age now. I think, on balance, that it would be jumping out of the frying pan into the fire.' Although there was a possibility of finding greater fulfilment and of working in a more congenial environment, her financial position and her general security were unlikely to be improved, and these were major considerations. Despite the disadvantages of her present job, she felt that she would do best to keep it.

Concluding Remarks

It is hoped that these two sample readings will give you an idea of how the cards are to be interpreted in a particular context. It will be seen that there is not a rigid meaning for each card, but that the basic meanings must be adapted to make sense when the cards are read in combination with one another and applied to the context of the Querent's personal situation.

Once you have acquired an understanding of most of the cards and have had experience of doing several readings, you may find it helpful to return to these sections and look at the examples again, as they will make more sense when you have begun to have experience as a Tarot reader and have already encountered some of the problems involved in interpreting a spread.

CHAPTER THREE

THE MAJOR ARCANA

The sequence of cards in the Major Arcana is often said to represent a journey of the soul, from the innocence of childhood, through various trials and ordeals, to maturity, old age, death, resurrection and spiritual transcendence. Some commentators see it as a series of stages in a process of initiation leading to enlightenment, resembling the initiation procedures of secret societies and the ancient mystery religions.

Another generally accepted view is that the cards of the Major Arcana represent archetypes — that is, symbolic figures which appear in the mythology, religions and folk tales of cultures all over the world and which occur in dreams and fantasies of people who have never consciously learned about them. The reason that these figures recur universally is because they are meaningful to everyone simply by virtue of our being human. They include, for instance, such figures as the Mother, the Father and the Wise Old Man, which have been associated with the Tarot cards of The Empress, The Emperor and The Hermit respectively.

In a Tarot reading, Major Arcana cards tend to signify underlying influences in the Querent's life, and circumstances beyond the control of the individual, which may be loosely understood in terms of fate or destiny. These cards can also relate to a deeper, spiritual level of experience beneath the superficial level of day to day events, and so may describe something of which the Querent is not consciously aware before it is pointed out during the reading.

In this chapter, we have explained some of the more common symbolism which appears in many versions of the cards, showing how it relates to the divinatory meanings.

0 The Fool

Traditionally this card depicts a beggar or a medieval court jester, but modern designs often show an attractive young man or a child. Sometimes he is on the edge of a precipice or in the company of wild animals, but these dangers seem not to trouble him, and he exhibits an air of carefree abandon.

His childishness represents trust and innocence; as a beggar, he is outside the constraints of normal society and free of worldly responsibility; as a court jester, he has licence to make fun of the royal court with impunity. His proximity to the precipice and the wild animals shows his willingness to take a risk. His bundle can be seen as representing his past experience: it is often said to symbolise the experience and karma of past lives, which will influence his future, even though he is not consciously aware of what the bundle contains.

In a reading, The Fool represents excitement, enthusiasm and a carefree attitude. It suggests the ability to live one day at a time without unnecessary worry about the future. Being like a child, in the positive sense of being spontaneous, trusting, and having an open mind, is also indicated. The card often appears in a spread when the Querent is engaging in a new venture, especially when an element of risk is involved.

KEY WORDS: Spontaneity, trust, taking a risk.

Reversed

Childishness in a negative sense is indicated when the card appears reversed. Reckless and impulsive behaviour is suggested.

Perhaps the Querent is acting foolishly on the spur of the moment without regard for the consequences. The reverse aspect of this card should be taken as a warning to be more cautious and to plan ahead. Possibly there is a reluctance on the part of the Querent to take on responsibility or to make commitments for fear of being tied down, but although this attitude may allow for enjoyment in the present, it is unlikely to be satisfying in the long term.

KEY WORDS: Recklessness, irresponsibility.

I The Magician

Old versions of this card show a man performing conjuring tricks, or perhaps selling trinkets from a stall. In modern versions he is a practitioner of the magical arts. An infinity symbol ∞ called a lemniscate may be above his head, or his hat may be suggestive of this shape. He is usually seen as embodying aspects of the masculine principle, such as rational thought and egoism.

Often he has one arm raised, the other hand pointing downwards, indicating that he is drawing power from above (mental and spiritual energy) to direct towards practical affairs (symbolised by the objects he is pointing to). These objects, especially in modern versions of the card, are usually a wand, a cup, a sword and a coin, representing the four elements of the material world; the Magician is master over them. As a conjurer he possesses skills of manipulation. In both the performance of tricks and in selling, a persuasive use of language may be involved.

When this card appears in a reading, it means that the Querent is confident, skilful and articulate, effectively directing his or her energy, creativity and imagination into practical matters. Independence of thought, willpower, charm, and good communication are also indicated. Now is the time to make use of these capacities and to put ideas into practice.

KEY WORDS: Skill, confidence, communication.

Reversed

The reverse aspect of this card indicates lack of confidence and a difficulty in putting ideas into practice effectively. There may be a breakdown in communication, or an unwillingness or inability to talk about some important matter, though it may not always suggest lack of ability so much as impediments to using the skills that one has.

Sometimes it can point to a misuse of these skills, where cleverness becomes cunning, and language is used to deceive and manipulate. Thus the reverse aspect of The Magician can be the confidence trickster or the person who resorts to emotional blackmail.

KEY WORDS: Lack of confidence, bad communication.

II The High Priestess

Traditionally this card is called The Papess (The Female Pope), but in modern decks is usually The High Priestess. Another version presents her as the goddess Juno. The title of The Papess seems to be a reference to the legend that one of the popes was a woman in disguise. Modern versions of the card often contain lunar imagery which identifies her with virgin moon goddesses.

Usually she is sitting between two pillars, called Boaz and Jakin, or Alpha and Omega, which represent the pillars in the temple of Jerusalem. One is black, signifying the passive feminine principle of the unconscious and mystery, and the other is white, signifying the active masculine principle of reason and consciousness.

The High Priestess is generally thought to represent those aspects of the feminine principle which are associated with deities of the moon and the underworld: darkness, mystery, dreams, the unconscious mind and intuition as opposed to conscious reasoning.

In a spread, this card signifies guidance, teaching or wisdom, particularly of a spiritual or moral nature, which comes from a mysterious source — often from the Querent's own unconscious mind in the form of dreams, fantasies or 'feminine intuition'. It can also represent an undeveloped inner potential, and possibly occult powers or influences. If the Querent is male, it may represent the feminine side of his personality, called the anima in psychology.

KEY WORDS: Intuition, dreams, anima.

Reversed

When reversed, this card suggests a lack of harmony with one's inner self. Feelings are being suppressed, and guidance or warnings from the unconscious ignored. Some potential in the Querent is not being recognised or has been denied an outlet, and particularly those qualities conventionally regarded as feminine are likely to be represented here.

In a man's spread the reverse aspect of this card may indicate negative feelings towards women, or that the Querent is not acknowledging the feminine side of himself.

KEY WORDS: Suppressed feelings, unrecognised potential.

III The Empress

This card often depicts a woman in a beautiful and fertile environment rich with fruit, flowers and ripe crops. Like that of The High Priestess, it represents aspects of the feminine principle, but whereas the High Priestess is associated with the virgin aspect, The Empress is the mother aspect. She may be seen as a personification of Nature, and is frequently shown as pregnant, to denote her fertility.

In a reading, this card indicates a pleasant, welcoming environment, a comfortable home, and satisfying relationships. Love, sex, marriage, childbirth and motherhood are all meanings which can apply to The Empress. Emotional as well as physical security is indicated, suggesting that the Querent has a strong sense of well-being and fulfilment which promotes generosity, kindness, a readiness to help others, and the enjoyment of company. Activities involved in home-making are also indicated.

KEY WORDS: Security, well-being, motherhood.

Reversed

The reverse aspect of this card often indicates domestic problems. Dissatisfaction with one's life, and a lack of material or emotional comfort may be indicated. Problems in relationships, such as the breakdown of a marriage, can also be signified.

Because of The Empress's association with childbirth, difficulties relating to pregnancy, such as miscarriage, unwanted pregnancy or abortion, are sometimes represented when this card appears reversed in a spread. In general, any problems regarding one's physical health or well-being, including poverty and homelessness, are possible interpretations.

KEY WORDS: Insecurity, domestic problems.

IV The Emperor

In contrast to the card of The Empress, The Emperor usually shows a barren and mountainous landscape. The figure of the Emperor himself looks stern and distant in most versions, and traditionally he is shown in profile, his gaze directed away from the viewer. His legs may be crossed in the form of a figure four, which stands for the material world consisting of four elements; this is the world in which the Emperor has dominion. He represents the father aspect of the masculine principle, and the power and authority which that entails.

In a reading, this card may represent the Querent, showing that he or she is a mature and rational person in a position of responsibility. The card often appears in a spread when the Querent is going to be promoted at work, or is moving to a job with better prospects.

More generally, it suggests that the Querent will be given the opportunity to exercise organisational abilities and to take control of a situation, perhaps one in which responsibility is assumed for other people's welfare.

KEY WORDS: Authority, responsibility, promotion.

Reversed

When the card is reversed, some issue concerning authority poses a problem for the Querent. Opposition to authority may be signified, or problems in relating to one's father. In a woman's spread, the reverse aspect of this card may indicate conflict with a domineering man.

In general, the Querent is likely to be found in a situation of being treated as inferior, or denied responsibility, which leads to resentment and a desire to rebel. Restrictions caused by petty rules and regulations may also be indicated.

KEY WORDS: Inferiority, restriction by rules.

V The Hierophant

Other names for this card include The Pope, The High Priest and Jupiter. A hierophant was an initiating priest and revealer of sacred mysteries in ancient Greece.

Some versions of this card feature a five-pointed star called a pentagram, which is a magical symbol of power and protection. It is also the symbol for humanity, because a human being possesses a body consisting of the four elements of matter, plus a mind, which add to five — the number of points on the pentagram. Furthermore, a human being has five extremities to the body — four limbs and a head — unlike most other animals which have a tail as well, making six.

There are usually two smaller figures in the foreground, representing people under the authority of the Hierophant who are receiving his teaching and his blessing.

Originally this card signified religious guidance and the teaching of the Church, but now that we live in a largely secular society, it is less likely to mean this when it appears in a spread. Instead of the priest, we have other authority figures to whom we turn for advice or learning, such as doctors, teachers, solicitors and personal counsellors, so when The Hierophant appears in a spread it probably indicates that the Querent is seeking professional advice from one of these sources. Occasionally it means that the Querent is giving advice in a professional capacity. Also, involvement in an educational establishment, either as a teacher or a student is sometimes indicated. When the card appears upright, the information from this professional source is helpful and reliable.

KEY WORDS: Professional advice, learning, teaching.

Reversed

Learning, teaching, or seeking professional advice is also signified by the reverse aspect of the card, but now there is a danger that the advice or information given is unreliable or not suitable for the Querent's needs. It may be that conventional advice and methods of dealing with problems are inappropriate in this case and that the Querent should find some other solution. On the other hand, the Querent may benefit from a second opinion if the first has proved unhelpful.

Occasionally the card appears reversed to indicate the severity of the problem on which the Querent is seeking advice, and does not necessarily mean that the advice will not be good.

KEY WORDS: Bad advice, misinformation.

VI The Lovers

Arthur Waite redesigned this card to depict Adam and Eve in the Garden of Eden in the presence of an angel. Modern decks based on the Rider-Waite often copy this theme, or show a young couple embracing. However, older versions are rather different, depicting a man apparently making a choice between two women while Cupid aims an arrow at his heart. Some versions show a marriage ceremony, or more than one couple are present. The theme of standing at a crossroads or a fork in the road is sometimes included.

The divinatory meaning of this card is usually concerned with matters of choice, rather than with love, which the title might suggest. The versions of the card which show the couple standing at a crossroads, and the traditional versions with the man flanked by two women, emphasise this interpretation. The Querent is faced with a difficult choice: taking one particular course of action forces rejection of others which may seem equally attractive, so there is a feeling of being drawn in different directions at once. There is also the problem that once the choice is made it will not be possible to go back on it because the Querent's life will have changed irrevocably.

Sometimes an important emotional commitment such as marriage may be signified, but more generally the choice is about any matter, such as changes in one's career, or moving home. When the card is upright it can be seen as reassuring the Querent that the right decision will eventually be made, though the matter may be worrying at present and deserves careful consideration.

KEY WORDS: Choice, decision, commitment.

Reversed

The Querent should be cautious in making an important decision, and weigh all the options very carefully. When this card appears reversed in a spread it can be a warning against making a hasty or ill-considered decision. Alternatively, the Querent may be postponing making a choice which seems too difficult to make, in the vain hope that problems will resolve themselves if ignored. In this case the Querent should start to consider taking some positive action and make a responsible decision rather than waiting for the difficulties to go away or for someone else to make the decision.

KEY WORDS: Indecision, bad decision.

VII The Chariot

This card traditionally shows a man in armour standing in a chariot drawn by two horses or sphinxes. Like the pillars on the card of

The High Priestess, in many versions one of these animals is white and the other black, representing the masculine and the feminine principles. Some modern decks replace the horses or sphinxes with other animals. For instance, in Aleister Crowley's Thoth deck, the chariot is drawn by four chimeras based on the appearance of the four Living Creatures of Ezekiel which often feature on other cards in the Major Arcana, notably The World.

The charioteer holds no reins, but guides the animals by willpower. They may be seen as aspects of his own psyche, and though they are opposing forces which would draw the chariot off its course if they were not controlled, the man is able to keep them in check and make them take him in the direction he chooses. This is an image of the power of the ego or conscious will over the rest of one's nature which is made subordinate to it. The philosopher Plato, in his dialogue the *Phaedrus*, uses this idea of a charioteer and two horses to represent the human soul (pp. 493 and 499, Hamilton and Cairns, 1963). According to Plato, the black horse represents our base instincts, while the white horse is our better nature.

When the card comes up in a reading, it shows that the Querent has a strong sense of direction in life and knows what he or she wants and how to get it. Ambition, drive, and the ability and will to surmount any obstacles in one's path are indicated. The fact that the charioteer is a warrior suggests that there may be conflicts ahead, both within oneself and with others, and there may be various problems to confront, but the upright position of this card in a spread implies that the Querent is well able to cope and has the skill, courage and determination to succeed.

KEY WORDS: Willpower, ambition.

Reversed

When reversed, this card represents what happens if the charioteer loses control of the animals drawing his chariot. The animals represent separate impulses in his own nature, so to lose control of them is to lose one's sense of direction and purpose. When this happens, one's life becomes either aimless or chaotic. Feelings of frustration are likely to turn to anger and a selfish disregard of the feelings of others as the Querent tries to be more self-assertive and to regain control, but this will only create more problems. A calmer, more organised approach is needed, trying to co-operate with others and to find ways to resolve problems rationally instead of confronting obstacles head-on.

KEY WORDS: Aimlessness, selfishness, inner conflict.

VIII Justice

In the Rider-Waite deck and some others, this card is number X. This is because the cards of Justice and Strength were transposed in the sequence of the Major Arcana so as to make the cards better fit the order of the signs of the zodiac which were attributed to them by the Golden Dawn and various commentators on the Tarot. Justice, with its scales, was associated with Libra, while Strength, depicting a lion, was associated with Leo. Leo comes before Libra in the zodiac, therefore the numbering of the cards Justice and Strength was altered so that Strength would be earlier in the sequence than Justice.

Justice, Strength (also known as Fortitude) and Temperance are three of the four Cardinal Virtues. The fourth one is Prudence, and is the only one not to appear in the standard Tarot pack. Traditionally, various virtues and other qualities have been personified as women. The usual representation of Justice in the Tarot is typical of this virtue, and has been a familiar image since medieval times. (The blindfold, which appears on some representations of Justice, is a later innovation which the Tarot image predates by several hundred years.)

In a reading, the card of Justice signifies that issues concerning justice and fairness are important, perhaps because the Querent is involved in a court case or has some legal problem. If Justice appears along with The Hierophant, for instance, this could represent a visit to the solicitor.

More generally, however, the card may represent any matter where the Querent is concerned that justice should be done. It often indicates a feeling that there is something unfair going on, which ought to be put right by rational discussion and arbitration, avoiding heated emotional argument. When the card is upright, this is a sign that reason and justice will prevail, that judgements will be made fairly and disagreements will be resolved. If there is a court case, it will probably be decided in the Querent's favour.

KEY WORDS: Justice, reason, legal matters.

Reversed

Unfairness, injustice and biased judgement are indicated when the card is reversed. It suggests that an unjust situation has persisted for some time and that there is little hope of its being resolved. Possibly this pessimistic outlook reflects the Querent's own feelings, and does not necessarily mean that the outcome will be bad. However, a different approach may be needed if the matter is to end favourably for the Querent.

If there is to be a court case, Justice reversed usually does not bode well, suggesting — if not an unfair outcome — at least delays and impediments to justice being done.

KEY WORDS: Injustice, bias.

IX The Hermit

The Hermit is usually portrayed as an old man dressed in a monk's habit and carrying a lantern. His environment often appears quite barren and inhospitable. In some versions, he has an hourglass instead of a lantern, suggesting that the image may originally have been intended to personify Time.

A hermit is someone who has deliberately withdrawn from society in order to dedicate himself to a life of quiet contemplation and prayer.

When this card appears in a reading, it indicates that the Querent feels a need to withdraw from a situation, due to either a dislike for what is happening, or a need for personal space and perhaps time to think. It indicates an independent attitude and the ability and desire to be self-reliant.

It can also represent an inner search and the desire for personal growth and self-development. Often it appears at a time of reassessment in one's life, after a period of great activity or stress, when rest and recovery are needed while one seeks a new direction. It suggests that the Querent needs to decide what should be done, without pressure or confusing influences from other people. Help from others is either undesirable or unavailable at this time. The Hermit indicates that solutions to present problems lie within and that one's deeper needs should be met.

KEY WORDS: Independence, solitariness, inner search.

Reversed

A desire to be independent and self-reliant is still indicated when the card is reversed, but now this attitude is inappropriate. The Querent may be struggling to cope alone when help is needed. This may be because no help has been offered, or the Querent has refused assistance.

This card can appear when the Querent feels isolated and excluded from relationships and social circles in spite of a desire to participate. Loneliness and self-pity are also indicated here.

Because of the hourglass in some versions of the card, the Querent's feelings about the passage of time may be relevant. Perhaps there is a resistance to change, reluctance to accept new ideas, or an inclination to morbid reminiscence and dwelling on what has been lost. If this is the case, a more positive attitude to the future needs to be adopted, and the Querent should seek out new interests and new friends instead of trying to live in the past.

KEY WORDS: Loneliness, exclusion.

X The Wheel of Fortune

Sometimes this card shows the wheel being turned by a woman representing the goddess Fortuna. Sometimes a sphinx — an emblem of feminine wisdom — presides over the wheel, to which various animals are clinging, or falling off. Some versions make an analogy with the card of The World by incorporating the four Living Creatures of Ezekiel which appear on that card. There may be esoteric symbols on the wheel, including the name of God (Yahweh) in Hebrew letters. Some modern versions prefer to depict Fortune in the form of the Three Fates or Norns.

In a spread, this card represents the workings of fate in the Querent's life. Chance occurrences or events beyond the control of the Querent are signified. When the card is upright, a period of good luck is indicated. This may be an unexpected turn for the better as past difficulties come to an end; or perhaps the Querent feels it is time for some good luck after an episode of misfortune. Sometimes it comes up in a spread when there is no particular course of action for the Querent to take in the situation because events will turn out for the best without human interference.

Occasionally it can indicate that the Querent's outlook on life is generally a fatalistic one with a tendency to believe in the forces of destiny, trusting that everything will be all right in the end, regardless of what decision is made! Surprisingly, such people sometimes do have more than an average share of good luck, so their optimism is not necessarily unrealistic.

KEY WORDS: Good luck, chance event.

Reversed

The Wheel of Fortune reversed signifies a period of bad luck. Misfortune may strike unexpectedly and everything seems to be going wrong despite the Querent's efforts to take control of what is happening.

Sometimes it can indicate that the Querent is a pessimistic fatalist, expecting misfortunes which are beyond one's control. This sort of attitude can be a symptom of depression, leading to further misfortunes which are actually unwittingly brought about by the depressed person. Other cards in a spread will indicate whether the bad luck signified here is merely a chance occurrence or whether the Querent can do anything to improve matters.

In any event, the message of this card is that one's fortunes change, so that after a period of bad luck, good fortune will eventually return.

KEY WORDS: Misfortune, pessimism.

XI Strength

As already explained, this card is sometimes number VIII in the sequence of the Major Arcana. Alternative names for it are Fortitude or Force. Aleister Crowley, in his Thoth deck, calls it Lust, apparently substituting a vice for a virtue, and illustrating it with the Whore of Babylon as described in the Book of Revelation.

The traditional image is either Hercules wrestling with the Nemean lion, or a woman taming a lion. The Hercules version seems to denote physical strength, when in fact it is moral strength and self-control which is represented here. The versions which show a woman holding the jaws of a lion are based on the traditional medieval personification of the virtue of fortitude; the lion was a conventional attribute of Fortitude in the same way as scales were a conventional attribute of Justice.

The lion may be seen as representing powerful emotions within the Querent — especially those which are often thought of as negative, such as anger or jealousy. When such feelings are suppressed they can become a dangerous force which undermines a person; on the other hand, if given free rein they can be just as destructive. In a well-balanced personality, the energy of these emotions is channelled into creative and positive activity, so that it becomes a source of strength.

The upright position of this card in a spread indicates that the Querent possesses this sort of self-control where nothing is suppressed, but a legitimate outlet is found for such feelings. It shows the ability of the Querent to cope in adversity by drawing on the inner strength provided by the energy of these emotions.

KEY WORDS: Moral strength, self-control.

Reversed

Lack of strength, and a feeling of being unable to cope is signified by the reverse aspect of this card. As with the upright meaning, the lion represents negative feelings, but now these feelings undermine the Querent who lacks the means to express them without causing offence. Emotional inhibitions and a lack of self-confidence lead to feelings of powerlessness. In fact the Querent is not as helpless as he or she would imagine, if only a way can be found of tapping the energy generated by taboo emotions and directing it towards some positive end, instead of using it to undermine oneself with self-blame and worry.

KEY WORDS: Helpless feelings, inhibitions.

XII The Hanged Man

The name of this card sometimes frightens newcomers to the Tarot, who imagine that it is a bad omen. The picture is certainly mysterious and does not offer any obvious interpretation. Some commentators in the past wanted to see The Hanged Man as being a representation of the Cardinal Virtue which is missing from the Tarot pack — Prudence — and suggested it was meant to portray a man standing on one leg. However, a little investigation shows this interpretation to be wrong. The figure is obviously hanging upside down, suspended from one foot, and this is apparent in the earliest surviving versions of the card.

Most versions of The Hanged Man show the man alive and with a contented or even blissful expression. Sometimes coins are falling out of his pockets, signifying renunciation of material things. Modern commentators usually see the picture as illustrating some sort of ritual sacrifice, and the self-sacrifice of the god Odin upon the World Ash in Norse mythology is often alluded to. Odin sacrificed himself in order to attain enlightenment, and thereby discovered the runic alphabet which is believed to have magical properties.

In a reading, therefore, this card signifies that the Querent is prepared to make sacrifices in life in order to achieve something which is of great personal value. It shows a desire to dedicate oneself to something worthwhile and personally fulfilling, even if other people see one as eccentric or irresponsible for so doing. What is sacrificed may be material comfort or one's reputation, but the Querent hopes to gain something which seems to be of far greater importance and which is likely to be of emotional or spiritual value.

Possibly the Querent has adopted a new outlook and now sees things differently from other people. This change is experienced as liberating, but it may be condemned by others who do not understand the Querent's altered values.

KEY WORDS: Sacrifice, dedication.

Reversed

Dissatisfaction, depression and apathy are indicated when the card is reversed. The Querent needs to find something of value and purpose in life, but at the moment this is lacking, and he or she does not feel enthusiastic about anything in particular.

Possibly the Querent is pursuing material goals at the expense of emotional or spiritual needs. Usually this is not intentional, but comes about because a person is trying to please others or to fulfil commitments which have been taken on. However, this situation cannot continue for long without serious detriment to the Querent's own sense of self-worth. There is a need to reorder one's priorities and to pay more attention to the things which one really considers to be fulfilling and worthwhile.

KEY WORDS: Dissatisfaction, apathy.

XIII Death

Traditional versions of this card personify Death as a skeleton wielding a scythe and reaping a harvest of dismembered bodies. This is a common medieval image, but to modern people it can seem gruesome and alarming. The Rider-Waite version and others based on it show Death as a horseman, as described in the Book of Revelation, which is perhaps a more tasteful and acceptable image; nevertheless this card can cause dismay when it comes up in a reading because the Querent is inclined to suppose that it is predicting physical death.

Only very rarely is actual death signified by the Death card, so the reader should be cautious of making this interpretation unless it is obvious — for instance, if the card appears in a position representing past events, and the Querent reveals that there has been a death in the family. In such a case, this may be backed up by the presence of other cards with a similar meaning, such as the Three of Swords.

If the Death card comes up in a position representing the future, however, the Tarot reader must never predict death; firstly because there is a very high probability of being wrong, and more importantly because the Querent will be quite unnecessarily distressed.

By far the most usual meaning of this card is radical change in the Querent's life: one phase of life has come to an end and a new one is beginning. The reason for this may be the sort of event which is usually a cause for celebration, such as marriage, starting a family, moving to a new home or starting a new job; but even though the changes may be desired they can still be stressful and it may be difficult to adapt.

When the card is upright, the Querent usually accepts the changes which are taking place and recognises them as inevitable. When past experiences have been painful, this card can signal changes for the better. Whatever these changes are, however, they are of such a nature that the past way of life will be lost forever, and the Querent has to accept this loss at the same time as embracing the new opportunities which the future brings.

KEY WORDS: Change, ending, new life.

Reversed

When Death appears reversed in a spread, it still indicates change of a radical nature, but now the Querent is resisting the changes taking place and experiencing them as more traumatic as a consequence. Perhaps the need for making changes has been held off until they become absolutely necessary, but by now they are more difficult to make.

Death reversed signifies a slow and painful period of transition, but in retrospect it will probably be recognised that these changes were necessary and, at least to some extent, beneficial.

KEY WORDS: Traumatic change, delayed change.

XIV Temperance

Usually this card depicts a winged figure pouring liquid from one vessel to another. The winged figures with which we are most familiar in art are angels, and so it has sometimes been supposed that the figure on the card of Temperance is an angel. The Rider-Waite deck, among others, depicts Temperance as the angel who announces the end of time in the Book of Revelation, and includes imagery from this source, such as a rainbow.

However, as mentioned earlier in this chapter, Temperance is one of the four Cardinal Virtues, and these virtues have traditionally been personified as women. The representation of Temperance as a winged female pouring liquid between two vessels is in fact a standard medieval image. The wings are a legacy from classical pagan traditions and do not mean that the woman is an angel, though it is likely that winged female figures of this sort inspired later Christian iconography.

Temperance has acquired the common meaning of abstinence — especially abstinence from alcoholic beverages. This, however, is not the meaning of temperance here. Rather, it refers to the practice of tempering something by mixing other substances with it. Temperance in this sense is finding the right balance or mixture. Sometimes one of the vessels the figure holds is gold, representing the sun and the masculine principle, while the other is silver, representing the moon and the feminine principle: the balanced personality has a harmonious blend of both. Other versions make references to alchemical practices in which one tries to transform base material into gold — a symbol for perfecting the self and raising it to a higher spiritual level. (In the Thoth deck, for instance, this card is called Art, meaning the art of alchemy.)

When Temperance appears in a spread, therefore, it indicates that the Querent has a mature and balanced personality and is able to handle a difficult situation with tact and efficiency. It suggests that the Querent may be in a situation where this cautious and balanced approach is required. Time should be taken to weigh up the best course of action.

Sometimes this card appears when the Querent needs to arbitrate between others in a dispute and it is necessary to maintain a detached and objective outlook.

KEY WORDS: Balanced personality, tactfulness.

Reversed

Imbalance and lack of self-control are signified by the reverse aspect of this card. It indicates swings of mood and feelings of uncertainty about what one really desires. Inconstancy of purpose and frequent changes of mind are indicated. Also, the Querent may be in conflict with other people and cannot cope with this without resorting to emotional outbursts. The clumsy handling of an awkward situation is a possible interpretation.

KEY WORDS: Moodiness, uncertainty.

XV The Devil

This is another card which sometimes frightens newcomers to the Tarot and which has led some people to suppose that the cards were the invention of the Devil and are under the control of demonic forces. In medieval times, however, it was common practice to represent the Devil and other demons in many different contexts: merely to portray the Devil was *not* believed to conjure up his presence, so we do not need to be afraid of this card.

The traditional image is of the Devil accompanied by two lesser demons in human form who are chained to the plinth on which he stands. Sometimes he is in the form of a goat. Modern decks occasionally try to remove the evil connotations by depicting a pagan deity generally known as the Horned God who is associated with fertility and nature worship. As on the card of The Hierophant, a pentagram sometimes features, but now it is inverted. The inverted pentagram is often regarded as a symbol of black magic, but this is a crude interpretation. More correctly, it represents the subordination of spirit and the higher functions of the mind (signified by the inverted pentagram's lowermost point) under the four material elements (signified by the other four points). This leads to materialism: the triumph of material values over spiritual values.

In a reading this card is unlikely to mean (as has been suggested by some commentators) evil, lust and demonic powers, since these extremes are not experienced by the average person seeking guidance from the Tarot. Instead, the card signifies the kind of bad things which are an unpleasant part of ordinary experience: anger, frustration, and being in uncomfortable circumstances from which one cannot escape.

The Devil can represent any situation which seems dark and depressing, but especially a situation in which the Querent feels trapped (like the figures chained to the Devil's plinth in the picture).

Anger and resentment are likely to be important features of the Querent's experience when this card appears in a spread — the sort of build-up of rage that occurs when one feels that there is no end in sight to an intolerable situation, and no outlet for one's emotions. This is only the Querent's subjective experience, however; possibly there are solutions to the problem which have not yet been explored.

KEY WORDS: Anger, oppressiveness, restriction.

Reversed

This card, when reversed, means much the same as its upright meaning, except that the oppressive and frustrating situation has probably continued for longer, so that now the Querent feels that some action to improve matters must be taken.

Often the Devil reversed appears when the Querent has already begun to make changes for the better, but the card represents the residue of bad feelings left after such a distressing experience.

KEY WORDS: Intolerable situation, escape.

XVI The Tower

Also called The Falling Tower, The Lightning-Struck Tower, or The House of God, this card usually depicts a tower being destroyed by a thunderbolt, its inhabitants hurtling out of the windows to their deaths. Sometimes one of the figures wears a crown, and the top of the tower which has been struck off is sometimes in a form suggestive of a crown too.

The crowns represent the Querent's ego or pride. This receives a sudden and unexpected blow which seems to the Querent to be a disaster. Shocking and disturbing events are indicated, especially those of a nature which lead one to re-evaluate oneself, one's lifestyle and relationships. Sometimes a physical accident can be signified.

These misfortunes, however, may be seen to be a blessing in disguise, for though such events are disturbing at the time they happen, something useful may be learnt from them. For instance, a shocking revelation may be unpleasant, but the information revealed may turn out to be helpful to the Querent. Likewise, circumstances surrounding an accident may provide an unexpected opportunity which the Querent would not otherwise have had.

KEY WORDS: Shock, revelation, accident.

Reversed

The shocking and humiliating nature of an unpleasant occurrence is somewhat diluted when the card is reversed. It is more likely to signify an undesired event which could have been foreseen or which has occurred gradually over a period of time. Sometimes it is a self-inflicted misfortune, or a problem which the Querent saw coming and took no steps to prevent.

Although this suggests less of a disaster, the positive aspects of the meaning associated with the card when it is upright do not apply when it is reversed. Thus, in its reverse position The Tower means a disappointment or a stroke of misfortune which is not especially severe but is also unlikely to bring any benefits in its wake.

KEY WORDS: Preventable misfortune, disappointing blow.

XVII The Star

The picture is usually of a beautiful naked young woman beside a pool, pouring water from two vessels onto the earth and into the pool. Behind her is an attractive landscape, often featuring a bird perching on a bush. Overhead is a large star surrounded by seven smaller stars which may represent the Pleiades or Seven Sisters.

The naked woman is generally thought to be a star goddess and is sometimes associated with the ancient Babylonian goddess Ishtar who ventured into the underworld on a quest for the water of life to restore her dead lover. Ishtar was known as the goddess of the heavenly waters.

When this card appears in a reading it signifies peace, rest and tranquillity. Problems are resolved and suddenly life is seen to hold unexpected blessings. Healing and a return to health in either a physical or spiritual sense may be indicated. The Querent experiences inspiration, refreshment and renewal after times of struggle and hardship. There is a feeling of quiet, inner calm, and a widening of horizons as the Querent becomes ready to try new experiences and adopt new solutions to old problems.

KEY WORDS: Peace, rest, healing.

Reversed

The opportunity for renewal, rest and healing is still present when the card is reversed, but the Querent is unaware of this. Anxiety, insecurity and lack of confidence may have become obstacles to appreciating the blessings in life, and there is a tendency towards pessimism.

The presence of this card in a spread is a sign of hope, showing that there is much to be enjoyed if only the Querent can adopt a more relaxed attitude and is not so fearful of the unknown. Although there may be obstacles to happiness, these can be overcome. The Star reversed represents the eventual attainment of fulfilment and peace, even if it is delayed.

KEY WORDS: Hope, delayed fulfilment.

XVIII The Moon

The traditional image is an eerie moonlit scene in which a path leads from a pool and passes between two dark towers. A crayfish, lobster or crab is crawling from the pool, and a dog and a wolf howl at the moon which has a woman's face, usually in profile. Other versions show astronomers gazing at the sky, or a man serenading his lover.

Commentators have associated elements of the traditional image with myths of the underworld. Cherry Gilchrist, in her book *Divination* (page 77), has pointed out that certain Babylonian boundary stones bear imagery which closely resembles that of The Moon card, so it seems that this may have a very ancient origin, the significance of which is now lost.

Like The High Priestess and The Empress, The Moon represents an aspect of the feminine principle. Goddesses have frequently been conceived of as being a trinity, corresponding to the waxing, full, and waning moon and representing the virgin, mother and crone phases of a woman's life. The High Priestess, as we have seen, is the virgin aspect of the feminine principle, and The Empress is the mother. The Moon now represents the crone, or old woman, and is often seen as having dark or negative connotations.

When this card appears in a spread, it signifies feelings of confusion, loneliness and lack of direction. The Querent has a feeling of groping in the dark with very little sense of what lies ahead. The crayfish emerging from the pool may be seen as fears surfacing from the unconscious mind. There may be feelings of depression and hopelessness.

The Moon is also a card of delusion and deception, so the Querent's feelings of being lost may be a result of being unable to see the true situation at the present time, either because of personal delusions or because of someone else's acts of deception.

Because of the moon's connection with the menstrual cycle, gynaecological problems are sometimes indicated.

KEY WORDS: Confusion, depression, deception.

Reversed

The problems related to the upright meaning of this card are probably more severe when the card is reversed. The sense of loneliness and depression is more marked, so the Querent may be approaching despair. Morbid fantasies, fears and phobias may also be indicated.

The Moon reversed is a sign that the Querent is in need of help and support because of a feeling of inability to face the problems ahead alone. The time has come to confide in a friend.

KEY WORDS: Fears, phobias, despair.

XIX The Sun

There are two common versions of this card. One shows twin children in a walled garden upon which the bright sun with a human face gazes down; the other is of a child mounted on a white horse. Both the twins and the white horse have been solar symbols since antiquity.

Just as the moon represents the feminine principle, the sun represents the masculine principle. When the card of The Sun appears in a spread, it signifies success, joy and personal achievement. It shows that the Querent has high ideals, is optimistic and ambitious, and possesses the energy to pursue personal aims and achieve important desires. It is one of the most auspicious cards in the pack and suggests not only ultimate success but also a sense of fun and excitement in the process of reaching that goal.

KEY WORDS: Success, optimism, high ideals.

Reversed

Some of the positive features of the meaning of this card still apply when it is reversed, but now there is likely to be a gulf between the Querent's ideals and what is possible to achieve at this time. A discrepancy of this sort can result in idle daydreaming and failure to engage in reality. There is also a feeling of disillusionment because one cannot attain what one wants.

More patience is needed, and the willingness to work towards realistic goals while enjoying what one already has. More ambitious aims can be pursued in the long term, with proper planning, and when the time is right.

KEY WORDS: Daydreaming, disillusionment.

XX Judgement

Traditionally this card depicts the Day of Judgement, with the dead rising from their graves at the call of an angel's trumpet. The fifteenth-century Visconti-Sforza deck shows God sitting in judgement in the sky. Some modern versions of the card have avoided this Christian imagery, however, using alternative symbols to convey the same ideas of regeneration and new beginnings. Crowley, for instance, has a completely different design and calls the card The Aeon, signifying the start of a new age.

When it appears in a spread, Judgement indicates that the Querent has been looking back on past events and assessing what happened. When the card is upright, the assessment is positive: the Querent feels sure of having done what was right, or what was best in the circumstances, and accepts the outcome as just or good. There is likely to be a feeling of satisfaction and achievement. Now the Querent can look forward to a new phase of life which is beginning.

KEY WORDS: Assessment, satisfying outcome.

Reversed

The end of one phase of life and the start of another is still signified when the card is reversed, but in this case the Querent looks back on what has happened with regret or remorse, wishing that he or she had behaved differently or that things had been otherwise. It may seem that matters have turned out unsatisfactorily and that the outcome is unfair. Often, however, this dissatisfaction or self-condemnation is unjustified because nothing could have been done to improve the situation, and now it is necessary simply to accept what has happened and look to the future.

KEY WORDS: Regret, remorse, unsatisfactory outcome.

XXI The World

This card is sometimes called The Universe. The traditional version depicts a dancing woman surrounded by a wreath of laurel leaves, and there are an angel, an eagle, a bull and a lion in the four corners of the card. This image is very puzzling, and perhaps for this reason some decks have a completely different version which is more easily explicable as a representation of the world or the universe.

The four creatures in the corners of the traditional image are known as the Living Creatures of Ezekiel, or cherubs. These creatures are first referred to in the Book of Ezekiel in the Bible, and then they appear again in the Book of Revelation. They can be seen as representing the four elements of matter, the four points of the compass, or the four fixed signs of the zodiac. Christians took them to represent Matthew, Mark, Luke and John, and they often appear in Christian iconography, sometimes surrounding the figure of Christ seated within a laurel wreath. Curiously, in the Tarot image, Christ has been replaced by a dancing figure, supposed by some commentators to be a hermaphrodite, and by others to be the anima mundi or world soul.

When this card appears in a spread, it signifies successful completion of a project, the end of one cycle or phase of life and the start of another, and the wholeness of the psyche. The Querent experiences a sense of fulfilment, peace and spiritual well-being. It suggests not only worldly success and the satisfying conclusion to any matter in hand, but points to something greater — a sense of freedom and elation which comes from growing self-knowledge and spiritual understanding.

KEY WORDS: Completion, spiritual wholeness, freedom.

Reversed

A pointless and frustrating circling of energy is indicated when The World is reversed. The Querent is in a vicious circle and is unable to break free of it. The same problems return, or the Querent feels stuck in a rut of boredom. A new approach is needed to prevent the same cycle of events from recurring.

Alternatively, action has already been taken to solve a problem or to bring some matter to its conclusion, but there are now delays and obstacles, and the Querent will have to wait a while before a satisfactory end is in sight.

KEY WORDS: Recurring problems, delayed completion.

CHAPTER FOUR

THE PIP CARDS

The 40 numbered cards of the Minor Arcana are called Pip cards because in traditional decks they are printed with the appropriate number of suit symbols, or 'pips', like playing cards, rather than having pictures on them. However, as we have explained earlier, modern decks often bear pictures on all the Minor Arcana cards, illustrating their meanings.

In contrast with the cards of the Major Arcana which, in a Tarot reading, tend to show experiences of a spiritual nature and forces operating beyond the Querent's control, the Pip cards tend to represent ordinary events in the Querent's life, and personal feelings about those events.

The Aces

The Ace of each suit stands for singularity or unity. It represents the full and undivided character and power of the element associated with the suit to which it belongs. The Ace of Wands represents fire; the Ace of Cups represents water; the Ace of Swords represents air; and the Ace of Coins represents earth.

Because the Aces are the first cards of each suit, they also represent the beginning of things: inspiration, new projects, new ideas, and birth (in either a literal or metaphorical sense).

Ace of Wands

This card embodies the energy and power of the masculine element of fire. It stands for inspiration, intuition, creativity, excitement, enthusiasm and ambition. It is a particularly auspicious card when the Querent is starting any new projects, or making career moves.

The suit of Wands is associated with career and business — with creative, organisational and intellectual aspects, rather than the practical or financial. The Ace of Wands shows that the Querent has the ideas, the ambition and the enthusiasm to succeed in activities engaged in.

KEY WORDS: Inspiration, enthusiasm, ambition.

Reversed

The creative energy represented by this card is misdirected when the card is reversed in a spread. The Querent is weak and drained, and does not know where to start or what to do first, feeling unenthusiastic, lacking in ideas, and frustrated through wasting energy on unproductive activities.

However, some of the qualities of the upright interpretation are still present, if only one can organise oneself more efficiently and decide what one really wants to do.

KEY WORDS: Wasted energy.

Ace of Cups

The feminine element of water is represented by this card. Water is associated with emotion, love, sensitivity, psychic powers and artistic gifts arising from the unconscious mind.

The Ace of Cups is an auspicious card for close personal relationships. It stands for love, joy and peace, contentment and emotional fulfilment. It shows that the Querent is a gentle and caring person who experiences love in relationships.

Specifically, it may signify a marriage, or the birth of a child. It can also represent the awakening of talents of an artistic or psychic nature.

KEY WORDS: Emotion, love, psychic powers.

Reversed

When reversed, this is a card of sadness, loss and despondency. The water now represents tears and melancholy. It indicates that the Querent feels a lack of love and emotional security and is in need of sympathy and comforting. An unhappy relationship may be signified, or loneliness and depression as a result of disappointments regarding love or marriage.

KEY WORDS: Sadness, loneliness, disappointment.

Ace of Swords

Swords represent the masculine element of air, which is associated with rational faculties and the intellect. The suit of Swords is also the suit most associated with conflict, destruction, power and painful loss.

Thinking is represented by a sword because, like a sword, it can be seen as cutting things up: we divide things into categories when we think about them, and when we make judgements and decisions. The Ace of Swords represents this ability to think clearly and rationally, and to make fair judgements and responsible decisions.

It also represents order and authority, and can stand for the sword of Justice, indicating that the Querent is concerned that justice should be done. Sometimes it can signify legal matters, indicating a fair outcome in a court case.

KEY WORDS: Intellect, reason, justice.

Reversed

When this card is reversed, it represents the misuse of the powers of the intellect, injustice, cruelty, clashes with authority, and possibly legal problems.

It may show that the Querent is trying to solve problems by rational means alone, without regard for feelings. It may show that the Querent believes that something unfair is happening and feels angry about this but powerless to do anything.

If a court case is signified, the card suggests that the outcome will be unfavourable for the Querent.

KEY WORDS: Cruelty, injustice.

Ace of Coins

The suit of Coins represents the feminine element of earth. Earth stands for material things, physical feelings and practical ability. It represents material and emotional security, money, fertility and work.

The Ace of Coins represents security, physical well-being, wealth and comfort. It can represent the Querent's sense of inner worth, a desire to help others, warmth and generosity, and the appreciation of beauty and of nature. It indicates that the Querent has a secure family life, enjoys the pleasures of the physical senses, and feels satisfied and content.

KEY WORDS: Feeling, security, wealth.

Reversed

Insecurity and a preoccupation with material things is signified by the reverse aspect of this card. It may represent a troubled family life, bad health, or worry about financial matters. Also it can represent a materialistic outlook, a lack of faith and spiritual awareness, and a fear of death or serious loss.

Alternatively it may show that the Querent feels anxious and disturbed, and is unable to appreciate the good things in life, or to enjoy life.

KEY WORDS: Insecurity, materialism.

The Twos

The number two represents the relationship and interaction between two entities, persons or principles. It may, for instance, represent the relationship between a man and a woman, or it may represent two different impulses or feelings within an individual person.

The relationship may be one of harmony and balance, or it may be one of conflict. The qualities associated with each suit of the Minor Arcana determine the meaning attached to the card numbered two in each particular suit.

Two of Wands

The Querent has reached a point at which a decision has to be made about what to do next. There has been partial success, or the completion of the first stage of a project, but the time has come to assess what one is doing and plan ahead.

The suit of Wands is associated with career, ambition and creative energy, so this card may indicate that the Querent needs to decide the direction a career should take. More generally, it can relate to any aims and ambitions which one has in life.

It can signify promotion or an improvement in circumstances, but this success may be accompanied by feelings of self-doubt and worry about what lies ahead, and there may be some inner conflict of desire.

KEY WORDS: Decision, initial success, self-doubt.

Reversed

When the card is reversed, the feelings of indecision and conflicting desires are stronger. One may be finding it difficult to recognise what has already been achieved, and now feels only disillusionment and a loss of momentum, and so begins to wonder whether one is doing the right thing. Perhaps something long hoped for has at last been attained, and now there is a feeling of anticlimax and wondering whether it has all been worth the effort.

This card can also represent falling out with a partner or business colleague.

KEY WORDS: Indecision, disillusionment, anticlimax.

Two of Cups

The suit of Cups is chiefly concerned with emotions and relationships, so the two of this suit represents the relationship between two people. Often it represents a love affair, engagement or marriage, but it can also represent a close and supportive friendship, or even a good business partnership. It shows that there is someone special in the Querent's life, whom the Querent is fond of and who can be trusted and relied upon, and that this is a relationship of equals.

Occasionally the card can appear in a spread when rivalry or disagreement with another person comes to an end and there is mutual forgiveness and tolerance.

KEY WORDS: Love, friendship, marriage.

Reversed

The reverse aspect of this card signifies problems in a relationship: quarrels, conflict and misunderstandings which lead to the breaking of an agreement. Divorce may be indicated, or the ending of an engagement. It suggests a clash of personalities which may make differences seem irreconcilable, but the Querent should beware of coming to a rash and hasty decision about ending a relationship, because this could be regretted later.

KEY WORDS: Quarrels, separation, divorce.

Two of Swords

Many of the cards in the suit of Swords represent conflict and the struggle for power. The two in this suit signifies the relationship between two opposing but equal forces so that an uneasy balance is maintained which may deteriorate into conflict at any time.

A disagreement between the Querent and another person may be indicated, or the conflict may be within the Querent's own psyche.

Often this card means that the Querent is trying to prevent discord, playing the role of peacemaker in a situation which has become very tense. However, the peace is maintained at present only by extreme caution and self-restraint, and arguments are likely to break out again before long.

KEY WORDS: Balance, peace restored, truce.

Reversed

When reversed, this is a card of conflict and injustice — sometimes even violence or cruelty. Differences of opinion in this situation are so strong that no common ground can be found, and the people involved have probably given up the attempt to be reasonable and moderate and are now simply giving vent to their feelings of anger and resentment, obstinately refusing to see one another's point of view. There is little hope of improvement, as the parties involved seem unlikely to be able to understand one another, at least while they are in this frame of mind.

KEY WORDS: Conflict, difference of opinion.

Two of Coins

Balance and equilibrium with regard to practical matters and emotional and material security is signified. The Querent has a practical and sensible outlook which makes everyday affairs run smoothly. Adaptable and able to cope with minor problems calmly and effectively, such a person has a happy, easy-going and accommodating attitude, enabling him or her to enjoy life from day to day and to remain optimistic despite changes and minor setbacks.

KEY WORDS: Practical ability, adaptability, harmonious change.

Reversed

When this card is reversed, the balanced and sensible attitude has given way to one of restless moodiness and inconstancy of purpose.

The Querent's mood fluctuates between happiness and misery; sometimes he or she feels confident, and sometimes unable to cope at all. Also there may be difficulty in maintaining concentration or interest in any one thing.

Reckless, immature or silly behaviour may be indicated.

KEY WORDS: Moodiness, fluctuation, silliness.

The Threes

The number three stands for the concept of creation. It symbolises the product of the union of opposites, in the way that offspring results from the union of male and female, creating a third person or animal where previously there were only two.

Also the number three can represent a link between two opposing forces, reinforcing the qualities of the relationship represented by the number two.

Three is the number of divinity and of fate, often regarded as a lucky number.

Three of Wands

Creative ideas with regard to business and enterprise are indicated. The successful start of any project may be signified, or the laying of plans for a new career or way of life.

After initial plans have been made, however, there may be a period of waiting to see how things develop from the processes which have now been set in motion by the Querent's initiative. To some extent, further success will be dependent upon luck, but there is every reason to be optimistic.

KEY WORDS: Creative ideas, laying plans, luck.

Reversed

The Querent knows what he or she wants, but is not sure how to get it. This leads to speculation about what might be done, but no steps are taken towards making dreams a reality. This may be because what is desired seems so far beyond what is attainable at this time, but on the other hand the Querent could be missing opportunities because of indecision and lack of confidence.

KEY WORDS: Procrastination, missed opportunities, unrealistic desires.

Three of Cups

Creativity within the emotional realm of the suit of Cups may signify the growth of a relationship, marriage, or the birth of a child.

This card suggests security, a comfortable home, a good family life, happiness and good fortune.

Alternatively, a birth or growth in a metaphorical sense may be indicated: spiritual or psychic growth may be represented here, or perhaps the Querent is engaged upon an artistically creative project which is close to the heart.

KEY WORDS: Growth, birth, marriage.

Reversed

Selfishness and intolerance within a personal relationship are indicated when this card is reversed. It suggests a relationship in which people engage because of what they can get out of it rather than what they can put into it. There is a lack of generosity, or even a tendency to use another person for one's own ends. This a pity, because there may be potential here for a good relationship, but this is being wasted.

Divorce, domestic problems, or problems regarding pregnancy are possible interpretations.

KEY WORDS: Selfishness, exploitation, domestic problems.

Three of Swords

Because the suit of Swords is concerned with conflict, power, intellect and ambition, many of the cards in this suit have unfortunate meanings. Within this context of power and conflict, the creativity and growth associated with the number three can only mean aggression, strife, destruction and the escalation of conflict.

The Three of Swords, therefore, signifies painful and difficult experiences, particularly sorrow associated with something coming to an end or being destroyed.

This card is similar in meaning to the Death card in the Major Arcana, and may indicate that distressing changes will make way for new and better experiences, but the process of change is likely to be unpleasant.

KEY WORDS: Sorrow, destruction, strife.

Reversed

When the card is reversed, a destructive and painful situation is likely to have persisted for some time. Arguments, hostility and hurtful behaviour are indicated.

This card is often reversed when something is coming to an end in a very destructive way, or over a prolonged period of time, creating bad feelings and a negative attitude which may lead to a desire for conflict and destruction for its own sake.

KEY WORDS: Prolonged conflict, pain, destruction.

Three of Coins

The creativity of the number three stands for gainful employment and the product of labour in the suit of Coins which is concerned with practical matters and security.

This card indicates that the Querent is working hard at something which is worthwhile and appreciated by others. This is a card of employment, or, more generally, doing work which satisfies the needs or requirements of other people, but the Querent also gains satisfaction from recognising that his or her work is valued.

KEY WORDS: Work, employment.

Reversed

When reversed, this card indicates that the Querent is doing a lot of hard work, but this is not as rewarding as it should be, either because other people do not appreciate the Querent's efforts and are critical or disapproving, or because there is not sufficient financial remuneration.

Sometimes it can indicate that the Querent's relationships with people at work are not good, or, more generally, the Querent may have a feeling of being taken for granted.

KEY WORDS: Unrewarding work.

The Fours

The number four is the number of the material world, which is composed of four elements and four dimensions — three dimensions in space and the fourth dimension of time. There are also four cardinal points and four seasons. Because of this association with matter, four stands for stability, firm foundations and order.

In combination with the masculine energy of the suits of Wands and Swords, four has a calming and stabilising effect, but in combination with the passive qualities of Cups and Coins, it tends to create too much stability, resulting in stagnation and restriction.

Four of Wands

The calm and stability of the number four represents a pleasant and restful environment in which the creativity and inspiration of the Wands energy can be freely expressed. This card, therefore, signifies freedom of expression and the pursuit of creative activities in an attractive, orderly and comfortable environment.

It may indicate that the Querent is going on holiday, providing an opportunity for this sort of experience. On the other hand, such experiences can also be found in creative work, or even in painting and decorating one's own home.

KEY WORDS: Free expression, creative work, holiday.

Reversed

The reverse aspect of this card signifies restriction on one's creativity and self-expression. The Querent is in an environment where rules and regulations are applied which are inhibiting and prevent free expression. He or she feels obliged to obey instructions and comply with the requirements of others, and does not feel happy about behaving naturally in such circumstances.

KEY WORDS: Restriction, regulations.

Four of Cups

In the gentle and passive suit of Cups, the stabilising influence of the number four creates dullness and apathy. One feels bored and stuck in a rut, and dissatisfied with what is happening even if one's experiences are generally desirable and one is doing things which one used to enjoy. Too much of a good thing can be boring in the end if there is no variety and nothing new happens, and there may be a tendency to take one's good fortune for granted. A change is needed, maybe in the form of a new, stimulating interest.

KEY WORDS: Apathy, boredom, excess.

Reversed

The Querent's boredom has degenerated into self-pity, self-indulgence and depression. There may not even be sufficient motivation to make the changes which are necessary to revitalise the Querent, having become apathetic, weary and fatalistic.

Sometimes problems such as drinking and eating too much, or indulging in drugs or alcohol may be indicated. It may be necessary for the Querent to seek help in overcoming problems and regaining a more positive outlook.

KEY WORDS: Self-indulgence, depression.

Four of Swords

The painful and destructive qualities associated with the Swords are removed by the pacifying influence of the number four. Therefore the meaning of this card is a respite from stress and trouble, and an opportunity to recuperate after a distressing experience or an illness. A holiday may be indicated, or a stay in hospital.

Alternatively, this card can simply mean that the Querent is finding time to rest and to attend to personal needs and interests, despite a busy and stressful way of life.

KEY WORDS: Rest from strife, recuperation.

Reversed

Isolation and a feeling of being shut out, rejected or banished are indicated when the card is reversed. Perhaps illness is preventing the Querent from engaging in the usual activities, or perhaps he or she feels rejected by people previously believed to be friends.

Occasionally the card signifies that the Querent has willingly left an undesirable situation, but there may still be a feeling of resentment that the circumstances were sufficiently bad to require this.

KEY WORDS: Banishment, rejection, escape.

Four of Coins

As the suit of Coins is already concerned with wealth and security, the additional influence of the number four, which signifies the material world, makes this a card of extreme stability and resistance to change. The Querent experiences material and emotional security, and feels that all personal needs are catered for. After times of difficulty, this may be very comforting, but if it persists for long and becomes a permanent way of life, the Querent could begin to feel stifled by the predictable and humdrum nature of his or her existence, and may grow over-cautious and unimaginative.

KEY WORDS: Stability, stifling security.

Reversed

This is sometimes said to be the card of the miser. This does not necessarily mean that one has a great deal of material wealth, but that in some sense one is clinging on to something which one has and is fearful of losing. This attitude may apply to a relationship, a job, or any aspect of the Querent's life, but can also apply to material possessions.

Fear of loss or failure may be making the Querent maintain a bad situation because he or she dreads making it worse by attempting change. In fact, this nervous and defensive attitude can make one feel more insecure, and there may be something to be gained by trying a different approach.

KEY WORDS: Possessiveness, miserliness.

The Fives

The stability of the number four is disrupted by adding the number one to it to make five. Five is the number of instability, hazard and struggle. The meanings of these cards, therefore, relate to conflicts, disappointments and the arrival of problems.

Five of Wands

The number five signifies arguments and obstacles here, but because of the optimism and enthusiasm of the Wands energy, the Querent is well able to deal with these problems.

Annoying incidents and minor set-backs are indicated, but these are likely to be ordinary, day-to-day problems which are a nuisance and which waste time, but which are not especially serious. In fact, the Querent may experience satisfaction in struggling with and overcoming these difficulties, which can add excitement and interest to life, and test one's skill in dealing with them.

KEY WORDS: Minor problems, struggle.

Reversed

More serious obstacles and disagreements are indicated when the card is reversed. Petty squabbling, arguments and rivalry may be signified, and there may be problems with a trouble-maker who intends to disrupt the Querent's plans. Some sort of power game may be taking place, but it looks as if one of the participants is not playing fair.

KEY WORDS: Rivalry, squabbling, disruption.

Five of Cups

The disruptive influence of the five, combined with the emotion of the suit of Cups, gives this card the meaning of disappointment and partial loss.

The Querent's cup of happiness has been upset, leaving the Querent dwelling upon what has been lost and feeling miserable, instead of appreciating what is still there. Being miserable and pessimistic is making problems worse than they need to be. It is still possible to salvage something from this situation, and to enjoy the good things that remain.

KEY WORDS: Partial loss, disappointment.

Reversed

The Querent has experienced a genuine loss which is causing sadness and distress. Something which was valued has gone from the Querent's life, leading to a feeling of bereavement in some sense, which will persist until the Querent comes to terms with the loss. There may be a sense of regret and remorse. These sorrowful feelings will lessen only with the passage of time.

KEY WORDS: Loss, remorse, sadness.

Five of Swords

The power and aggression of the suit of Swords, combined with the instability and conflict of the number five, signifies humiliation and defeat.

The Querent has a feeling of having been made to look small and inferior, or is embarrassed by personal weaknesses being exposed. He or she may have come into conflict with, and been overpowered by, a domineering or superior person.

Nothing can be done in this situation but to accept defeat gracefully, recognising that the opponent was too strong and had all the advantage. Rather than any substantial harm to the Querent, it is probably only pride which has been hurt.

KEY WORDS: Defeat, humiliation.

Reversed

The Querent has been hurt and humiliated by someone acting in a bullying or spiteful way. The meaning here is much the same as the upright meaning, but the unpleasant aspects are emphasised, and there may be deception or dishonesty involved. When the card is reversed it is more likely that the Querent has encountered a malicious person who deliberately intends to be hurtful.

KEY WORDS: Humiliation, bullying, deception.

Five of Coins

The disruptive effect of the number five in the context of the material and emotional security associated with the suit of Coins makes this a card of impoverishment and adverse material circumstances. Unemployment may be signified, or the Querent may have financial worries.

Alternatively, the poverty may not be material poverty, but a symbol for something that the Querent really needs but which is lacking at present, such as love, respect, or a steady relationship. However, help may be closer at hand than the Querent realises, and troubles will be alleviated by a companion who can share them.

KEY WORDS: Material trouble, poverty, worry.

Reversed

The Querent is acutely aware of the lack of something which is needed, and this situation has probably continued for some time. Severe financial problems, homelessness or long-term unemployment may be signified, or, more generally, the Querent feels a distinct lack of love and security. Continuing in the way that one is going at present is likely to lead to further problems which could otherwise be avoided.

KEY WORDS: Poverty, unemployment, destitution.

The Sixes

Harmony, balance and equilibrium are signified by the number six. According to the Bible, the world was created in six days, so six is also the number for effort which brings about a successful completion followed by rest. The sixes in the Minor Arcana, therefore, are concerned with balance, justice, rewards, and the consequences of past action.

Six of Wands

Past effort has resulted in success and achievement which can now be enjoyed. This is a card of triumph and victory: the Querent has patiently worked towards this moment, and now those efforts are recognised and rewarded. News of the successful outcome of any matter may also be signified.

KEY WORDS: Victory, triumph.

Reversed

Successful completion of a project is delayed, or goes without recognition. A time of triumph and celebration is deserved or expected, but turns out to be an anticlimax.

The reverse aspect of this card can also signify the delayed arrival of news that was hoped for earlier. Sometimes misunderstanding, or a lack of proper communication, is involved.

KEY WORDS: Anticlimax, delayed success.

Six of Cups

The suit of Cups concerns emotions and relationships, so the rewards of past actions signified by the number six apply, in this suit, to the rewards of past friendships and acts of kindness.

The Querent may be thinking about happy times in the past, or of childhood experiences, and this reminiscence brings pleasure and comfort in the present. Alternatively, an old friend or lover may return unexpectedly and repay a past act of kindness by helping the Querent with present needs.

KEY WORDS: Pleasant memories, old friends, childhood.

Reversed

The Querent is haunted by an unhappy past, or is living in the past at the expense of enjoying the present. Nostalgic feelings, the regret that good times have gone by or that a relationship has ended, are preventing the Querent from making the best of life at the moment, and may be a way of avoiding facing present issues.

KEY WORDS: Unhappy memories, nostalgia.

Six of Swords

The harmonious influence of the number six has the effect of moderating the struggle and suffering associated with the suit of Swords. This card indicates that the Querent is moving away from times of trouble and faces better prospects for the future.

There is a slightly melancholy atmosphere about the Six of Swords, suggesting that not all the Querent's problems will be resolved at once, but it generally indicates an improvement in circumstances, the ending of sorrow and worry, and can sometimes represent a physical move to a new home, or a journey abroad.

KEY WORDS: Improvement, passage, journey.

Reversed

The Querent has taken temporary measures to solve a problem, but a permanent solution has not yet been found or has been avoided, so the same troubles are likely to resurface later. The Querent may be trying to take the easiest course of action, but a more lasting solution is needed.

KEY WORDS: Temporary improvement.

Six of Coins

Balance and justice with regard to money and security are signified by this card. The sharing out of money or possessions, or the giving and receiving of gifts may be indicated.

More generally, the Six of Coins means that the Querent is a generous person who likes to help others and to show care and affection. An act of charity or the payment of a karmic debt are also possible interpretations.

KEY WORDS: Gift, charity.

Reversed

The Querent feels cheated or as if something has been stolen. It may be that other people have taken advantage of the good nature of the Querent who is doing all the giving while others do all the taking. The situation seems unfair, and the Querent feels that his or her generosity has not been appreciated.

Alternatively, theft, or the loss of money or possessions may be indicated. The Querent's own gullibility or carelessness may have contributed to this situation.

KEY WORDS: Theft, being cheated or used.

The Sevens

Seven is considered a lucky or magical number and is associated with wisdom, supernatural powers, fate and morality. There are Seven Virtues and Seven Deadly Sins, Seven Pillars of Wisdom, seven days of the week, seven colours in the rainbow and seven notes in a musical scale. In many cultures, seven is a number of great mystical power, and these special powers of the number seven attach to the meanings of the sevens in the Minor Arcana, which are concerned with special skills or gifts associated with the qualities of each suit.

Seven of Wands

The wisdom and power of the number seven, in combination with the enthusiasm and ambition of the Wands, signifies the ability to overcome obstacles and to meet a challenge with courage and the determination to succeed.

The Querent may be facing a test of some nature, such as an examination, a driving test or a job interview. On the other hand, a challenge or test in a more general sense may be signified. The Querent faces a situation in which skill and resilience are needed, and is well able to cope, maybe even deriving satisfaction from this chance to exercise these qualities.

KEY WORDS: Challenge, test, valour.

Reversed

The Querent faces a test or challenge, but feels unable to meet it. This is not so much through a lack of ability, but through a lack of the necessary confidence. Shame and self-condemnation at one's own failure of courage only exacerbates the problem. The Querent may actually be more capable than he or she has admitted in the past.

KEY WORDS: Failure to meet a challenge, lacking confidence.

Seven of Cups

The special powers and abilities signified by the number seven in the suit of Cups are imaginative and psychic powers, and ideas arising from the unconscious. These are valuable gifts, but there is a danger that, unless tempered by reason, they may lead the Querent astray into the realms of fantasy.

Here, the Querent contemplates a number of ideas, dreams or fantasies relating to hopes and aspirations. It is necessary to choose between these various options, deciding which ideas are realistic and worth pursuing, and which are hopeless daydreams. All the options are tempting, so the Querent must be careful and rational in making the choice.

KEY WORDS: Fantasy, illusion, choice.

Reversed

The Querent is bewildered and mesmerised by the number of possibilities which the future seems to hold. Reluctant to make a decision, the Querent retreats into fantasy, dreaming about what might be done, but failing in self-application or to make definite plans. There is a danger that the Querent is deluded and that none of these present ideas are realistic. A more rational and practical approach is needed.

KEY WORDS: Delusion, fantasy, bewilderment.

Seven of Swords

In the suit of Swords, the number seven signifies the intelligence, cunning and foresight which are the special skills of this suit. The card indicates that the Querent has a chance of using intelligence to deal with a problem — especially one involving powerful opposition — in a clever and skilful way by forestalling trouble, taking precautions and avoiding direct confrontation. In this way, a potential opponent is disarmed in advance, and conflict is avoided.

Unorthodox, evasive or even eccentric behaviour is indicated, but it will bring the results the Querent wants.

KEY WORDS: Foresight, evasion, disarming the opposition.

Reversed

An unorthodox, individualistic course of action would be of benefit at this time, but the Querent feels too timid to take advantage of the opportunity available. Fear of disapproval or of appearing eccentric results in a conservative, extremely cautious stance, but this may lead to problems later on as a chance is missed to forestall trouble.

KEY WORDS: Timidity, conservative behaviour.

Seven of Coins

In the suit of Coins, the number seven emphasises practical ability, perseverance and hard work which are the particular skills associated with this suit.

The Querent should not feel discouraged by present setbacks, because sustained effort will bring success. Circumstances may look unfavourable, but the Querent will soon see the results of such hard work, and may enjoy a stroke of good fortune very soon.

KEY WORDS: Perseverance, discouraging cicumstances.

Reversed

The Querent feels despondent, and inclined to abandon a project presently engaged upon, because the desired results have not been achieved. Opportunities have been missed, and the Querent may have brought about self-inflicted problems by not taking the initiative when the chance was available. Matters have been allowed to deteriorate to such an extent that failure probably cannot be avoided now. The Querent would do best to cut any losses and learn from this experience not to make the same mistakes again.

KEY WORDS: Despondency, failure, abandonment.

The Eights

The number eight is produced by multiplying four by two. It therefore contains the stability and material security of the four, and the balance and movement of the two. Eight is the number of material success and justice, but it also contains the idea of progress and development.

The meanings of the eights in the Minor Arcana therefore concern the idea of establishing secure foundations but then progressing from that point towards further personal growth and greater success in the future.

Eight of Wands

The energy of the Wands suit, combined with the notions of success, justice and progress associated with the number eight gives this card the meaning of swift progress towards a successful conclusion of any matter in hand. There will be an end to delays, and processes initiated by the Querent will take on a momentum of their own, leading to a desired result. There will be much excitement and activity as developments which the Querent has hoped for begin to come about.

KEY WORDS: Swiftness, activity, rapid conclusion.

Reversed

There is much feverish activity, but little is achieved. Events happen too quickly for the Querent to cope with, and energy is wasted and exhausted in trying to keep up. Things happen in the wrong way at the wrong time, there is disorganisation and lack of planning and co-ordination. The Querent is losing control of the situation and is taken by surprise by unexpected developments.

KEY WORDS: Haste, disorganisation, exhaustion.

Eight of Cups

The ideas of security, success and progress associated with the number eight apply to the Querent's relationships and emotional well-being when the Eight of Cups appears in a spread.

The Querent has enjoyed a situation or relationship where there was stability, peace and security, but this is not enough. Something seems to be lacking in life and it is time to move on to new things. Although this means leaving behind much that is satisfying and enjoyable, and abandoning something which was already established, the Querent recognises that personal development is dependent upon making this sacrifice.

New relationships, new friends, a new job or a new home are all possible interpretations.

KEY WORDS: Moving on, personal development, sacrifice.

Reversed

The Querent feels like making big changes in life and moving on to new things; ending a relationship, changing jobs or moving home, may be the sort of idea under consideration. However, there is danger here of making a bad mistake and abandoning something which is safe and reliable for something which is risky and may turn out to be a complete fantasy.

Perhaps the Querent's present circumstances have more to offer than is apparent at the moment, and it may be possible to make improvements without resorting to drastic changes which could later be regretted.

KEY WORDS: Abandoned success.

Eight of Swords

In the suit of Swords, the adverse influence of the Swords impedes the progress and development associated with the number eight.

The Querent would like to make changes and improvements, but is, instead restricted and hemmed in. Only small improvements are possible at this time, but the Querent should pay attention to detail: some small opportunity may be available which has been missed, and slight progress is better than none at all. Patience is needed; the situation may not be as difficult as it seems.

KEY WORDS: Restriction, impediment.

Reversed

Feelings of restriction and impediments to progress and improvement are stronger when the card is reversed. The Querent feels helpless, unable to act. However, the situation has probably become as bad as it can get, and changes will have to happen soon, if only because the Querent becomes desperate enough to take a course of action which forces developments to come about.

KEY WORDS: Great restriction, need for change.

Eight of Coins

The achievement and progress of the number eight, together with the practical ability and material and emotional security of the Coins, signifies prosperity, and satisfaction from work. This may be work which requires a special skill or craftsmanship, or perhaps the Querent is self-employed. Alternatively, the Querent may be engrossed in a hobby or personal project which brings much pleasure.

Whatever activity is indicated, the Querent receives more than material or financial gain from it: there is a sense of pride, personal satisfaction and achievement derived from the exercise of one's skills and in seeing that the work has been done well.

KEY WORDS: Skilled work, crafts, self-employment.

Reversed

The Querent is unable to concentrate on work of a satisfying nature or to any long-term projects because the concerns of the present moment always take priority. Worry about doing one's duty, making money or being secure in the short term prevent the Querent from planning for the future and following up personal ambitions. In fact this can mean wasted efforts in order to secure small and transitory gains, whereas the Querent's real interests would be better served by planning ahead for greater security and prosperity in the future.

KEY WORDS: Short-term gain, expediency.

The Nines

As the final single-digit number, nine represents completion or the final stage. Nine is produced by multiplying three by three, so it contains the creative power of the number three, tripled to signify attainment on material, intellectual and spiritual levels simultaneously. Unlike the number three, which is associated with creativity in the initial stages, the number nine represents creativity in the context of achieving results and benefiting from former effort and experience.

Nine of Wands

The achievement of results and benefit from past experience signified by the number nine indicates determination to succeed against all the odds when combined with the force and dynamism of the Wands.

The Querent has experienced problems, obstacles and suffering, and has had to fight to attain the present position, but remains undaunted and possesses the courage and will to carry on in spite of opposition and the anticipation of further trouble. What has already been achieved places the Querent in a strong position from which to advance, despite feeling wary and defensive, having learned from past suffering to be cautious now.

KEY WORDS: Strength, courageous persistence.

Reversed

Obstinately battling on with a hopeless situation is indicated when the card is reversed. The Querent is reluctant to admit defeat and so persists in a course of action which is unlikely to bring the desired results. Having been hurt in the past, the Querent is now suspicious and defensive, reluctant to make compromises or changes in approach. This will only create tension in interactions with others, and nothing is to be gained. The Querent needs to be more flexible and to adapt to changing circumstances.

KEY WORDS: Obstinacy, futile persistence.

Nine of Cups

The achievement and continued creativity of the number nine signifies, in the suit of Cups, contentment and a hospitable, generous nature.

Having attained personal happiness and a sense of well-being, the Querent now wishes to share this joy with others. An optimistic and caring attitude is indicated; love, friendship, good company and comfortable surroundings. There is much to enjoy, and the companionship of family and friends brings the Querent especial pleasure.

KEY WORDS: Happiness, optimism, hospitality.

Reversed

The reverse aspect of this card represents complacency and smugness. The Querent feels safe, secure, and satisfied with present circumstances, but all may not be as good as it seems.

Perhaps the Querent is not as popular as he or she believes, or has placed too much trust in the surface appearance of things. A deeper and more questioning examination of self, of relationships and of the general situation may reveal problems which the Querent is inclined to overlook because of false optimism or overconfidence.

KEY WORDS: Complacency, superficiality.

Nine of Swords

As with many cards in the suit of Swords, the Nine of Swords has a rather unfortunate meaning. The creativity and influence of past experience, associated with the number nine, is turned to worry and sorrow here.

The Querent has suffered in the past and cannot escape from the negative influence of these experiences. Anxiety — especially over what other people are thinking and doing behind one's back — despair and misery are indicated. The Querent may be having bad dreams, or is unable to relax because of nervousness and depression.

This is a card of mental anguish; the Querent dreads what will happen, but pessimism and morbid fantasies are making the situation seem worse than it really is.

KEY WORDS: Despair, depression, mental anguish.

Reversed

Persistent depression and anxiety are indicated when the card is reversed. The Querent is weighed down by morbid fantasies, despondency and fear. This state of mind is making it difficult to cope, creating more problems, and help from others may be needed to bring about an improvement. At present, however, the Querent may suspect that others are hostile, behaving cruelly, or persecuting him or her in some way. This suspicion could be justified, but the Querent's problems are only exacerbated by this negative outlook. Sometimes clinical depression is signified.

KEY WORDS: Severe depression, cruelty, morbid fantasies.

Nine of Coins

In the suit of Coins, which is concerned with material success and emotional well-being, the achievement attached to the number nine signifies security, peace and comfort which have been earned by past effort and which are well-deserved.

There has been a great deal of struggle and sacrifice in order to attain this present situation, and it is now time to relax and enjoy the fruits of one's labours. Past hardship may make the Querent appreciate any present advantages all the more, though there could be an underlying fear that this good fortune may not last for long.

This card often represents someone living alone, enjoying personal achievements in solitude and privacy, but this does not necessarily imply loneliness: solitude may be one of the features of the circumstances which the Querent values most at this time.

KEY WORDS: Material gain, security achieved through effort.

Reversed

The Querent's prosperity and comfort are not as secure as it would appear. Possibly the Querent has a guilty conscience and fears that past misdeeds will come to light, undermining present fortunes. On the other hand, the Querent's security may not have been the result of personal efforts, but due to someone else on whom the Querent is dependent. This lack of independence may lead to feelings of insecurity because the Querent is not in control.

KEY WORDS: Illusory security, dependence.

The Tens

Our system of numerals has the number ten as the base: that, is, we number from one to nine and then begin the sequence of two-digit numbers, using the same numerals as before. Ten, therefore, represents the beginning of a new stage of development.

Ten is also thought of as a number of completion, but it can be seen as going beyond what is required for completion, leading to the idea of one too many, decadence or destruction. These concepts relate to some of the meanings of the tens in the Minor Arcana. The number ten here can also signify a group of people.

Ten of Wands

The idea of over-completion and 'one too many', associated with the number ten, is relevant here. As the suit of Wands is concerned with ambition and initiative, this card signifies that the Querent is very busy, involved in a number of different projects at once, and taking on many responsibilities. However, there is a risk of trying to do too much, or taking on responsibilities which really belong to others. Some activities may be coming to a conclusion now, so the Querent should be careful about how many new commitments are taken on.

KEY WORDS: Burden of responsibility, many commitments.

Reversed

The Querent is trying to do far too much at once and is becoming confused and exhausted by the burden of commitments. There is a danger of becoming inefficient because of spreading one's resources too thinly.

The Querent needs to decide what is most important and concentrate on that, giving up some other activities which are less important or which could be done by other people who are able to share the Querent's responsibilities.

To some extent the Querent may be responsible for this problem through reluctance to delegate tasks to others and trying to take on everything personally.

KEY WORDS: Oppressive burden, overwork.

Ten of Cups

The number ten may represent a group of people here. As with the other cards in the suit of Cups, this one is about emotions and personal relationships.

Happiness, contentment and the fulfilment of one's deepest wishes are indicated, particularly in the context of family life or enjoying oneself with a group of friends.

When the card is upright, this favourable meaning generally applies, but, as already mentioned, the number ten can signify decadence or too much of something, so there is a possibility that one of the people in the Querent's family or social group is not as contented as everyone else, and this may mar an otherwise idyllically happy situation.

KEY WORDS: Fulfilment, joy, happy family.

Reversed

An annoying, disruptive event, or the behaviour of a particular individual in the Querent's family or group of friends, disturbs an otherwise happy and peaceful situation.

Perhaps one person in a social group is dissatisfied and has problems, and is, therefore awkward to get along with, while other people cannot understand the problem, so the individual is seen as a trouble-maker. Alternatively, someone may be used as a scapegoat for the frustrations of the rest of the group. This person may be the Querent, or a close friend or relative.

KEY WORDS: Disrupted happiness, disgruntled individual.

Ten of Swords

The ideas of completion and a group of people, associated with the meaning of the number ten, take on rather negative connotations in the suit of Swords.

The Querent should beware of getting involved in a group of people whose problems will cause trouble for the Querent, though this may not be possible if they are members of one's own family or people to whom one has a commitment.

However, as the number ten also signifies the conclusion of something and the beginning of a new phase, this card can indicate that problems, conflict and pain are coming to an end and that the Querent is now experiencing the worst point of a crisis, after which the situation will improve. This is sometimes described as a card of ruin and disaster, but it also offers hope for a brighter future.

KEY WORDS: Crisis, ruin, unlucky group of people.

Reversed

A bad situation is likely to grow worse. It may look as if troubles are coming to an end, but this is probably an illusion. The crisis point has not yet been reached, so the Querent ought to be prepared for further trouble and not rely on false hopes which only lead to further disappointment. As with the upright meaning, a group of people could be involved.

KEY WORDS: False hope, continuing misfortune, ruin.

Ten of Coins

The group of people signified by the number ten is usually the Querent's family in the Ten of Coins, although a group of friends could be represented.

As Coins is the suit of security and wealth, this card stands for family support — either emotional or financial. It indicates that the

Querent is part of a close-knit family or a supportive group of people which provides help, security and advice when needed, but in return the Querent has certain responsibilities towards these people. When the card is upright, there is usually mutual benefit.

Another possible interpretation is the influence of one's background and upbringing upon one's present attitudes, values, behaviour and way of life; again, when the card is upright this is probably a good influence.

Sometimes inherited money is indicated.

KEY WORDS: Family support, friends, inheritance.

Reversed

Harmful influences from one's family, friends or upbringing are indicated when the card is reversed. There may be interference from members of the family or close friends who are giving advice the Querent does not want.

Alternatively the Querent may be burdened by the problems of friends or family members. The difficulties of being in a group of people which stifles the Querent's individuality and imposes worrying responsibilities may be signified.

Sometimes the reverse aspect of this card indicates problems and conflicts arising from an inheritance.

KEY WORDS: Family problems, social responsibility.

CHAPTER FIVE

THE COURT CARDS

Traditionally the Court cards of each suit of the Minor Arcana are called Page, Knight, Queen and King. In some modern decks, one of the male cards — usually the Page — is renamed the Princess in order that there should be two Court cards of each sex in each of the four suits of the Minor Arcana. In these decks, the names are usually Princess, Prince, Queen and King. In the Golden Dawn and the Thoth Tarots, however, the Kings are called Princes, so the sequence is Princess, Knight, Queen and Prince. In some modern decks, the Court cards have completely different names, so you need to be sure which traditional cards they correspond to when referring to the meanings in this book.

In a Tarot reading, the Court cards are generally thought to represent particular individuals — either the Querent, people known to the Querent, or people he or she is going to meet.

Because the Court cards are part of the Minor Arcana, like the Pip cards they are in suits, and the elements associated with the suits affect the personalities of the characters depicted. The Court cards in the suit of Wands, therefore, are influenced by the element of fire, which makes them, on the whole, lively, extroverted characters, while the Court cards in the suit of Cups are under the influence of the element of water, which makes the characters they depict rather quiet, introverted and inclined to daydream. Likewise, the Court cards in the suit of Swords represent intellectual people who depend very much upon rational thinking, since these qualities are associated with the element of air; and the Court cards in the suit of Coins take on the practical, common-sense qualities associated with earth.

In connection with this idea, it is often said that the Court cards in the suit of Wands represent people born under the fire signs of the zodiac (Aries, Leo and Sagittarius); those in the suit of Cups represent people born under water signs (Pisces, Cancer and Scorpio); those in the suit of Swords represent people born under air signs (Gemini, Libra and Aquarius); and those in the suit of Coins represent people born under earth signs (Taurus, Virgo and Capricorn). This is not always the case, however, so it is best not to apply the rule too strictly, though some readers who are already familiar with astrology may find it a helpful guideline. You may also wish to know the astrological attributions of the Court cards if you are using a Significator — a card to represent the Querent, which is removed from the deck at the start of a reading and which serves as a focus for the Tarot reader's attention while the cards are being shuffled and selected.

If you wish to use a Court card as a Significator, another way to choose an appropriate card is on the basis of the Querent's hair and eye colouring. Court cards in the suit of Wands are said to represent people with blond or red hair and blue eyes; those in the suit of Cups represent people with light brown hair and blue or hazel eyes; Court cards in the suit of Swords represent people with dark brown hair and brown eyes; and people with black hair and dark skin, or those with white hair, are represented by the Court cards in the suit of Coins.

It can be difficult to interpret Court cards when they appear in a spread, because sometimes they represent, not individual people, but situations; and occasionally they represent both a situation and a person involved in that situation. To decide which is appropriate in a particular reading, it may be necessary to try out more than one interpretation. The Knights and Pages are the Court cards most likely to represent situations, so for each of them we have provided an interpretation for a situation as well as for an individual's personality, allowing you to choose which is most suitable.

The Pages

These cards are sometimes called Princesses or given some other feminine title, as explained above, or they are called Pages but depict girls. If a Page comes up in a reading, it may represent a child of either sex, a young woman, or a situation. All the Pages correspond to the element of Earth, signifying foundations, practical matters and the initial stages of any project.

Page of Wands

Personality This is a lively, sociable person with plenty of energy, who will bring fun and excitement into the Querent's life and make a faithful and reliable friend. This person is witty and resourceful, enjoys having a chat, and may be the bearer of good news.

Situation If the card represents a situation, it shows the Querent engaging in some new activity with energy, enthusiasm and resourcefulness. Also, new opportunities and good news may be signified.

Reversed

Personality A rather shallow, dull and self-opinionated person is represented who tries to be friendly and amusing, but is more likely to be a nuisance, because of an inability to respect privacy and keep a secret. This person is unreliable and may give misleading information or spread gossip.

Situation Bad news may be signified, or possibly the delayed arrival of good news. The reverse aspect of this card can also represent lethargy, and being easily discouraged in the face of obstacles.

Page of Cups

Personality A quiet, introverted and studious person is signified — especially someone who has artistic or psychic gifts. This person may assist the Querent if asked to help, but is probably too shy to offer help if not asked, being very sensitive and modest, and perhaps hiding his or her true skills.

Situation Latent skills and talents in the Querent may be represented by this card. Artistic and psychic ability may be indicated, and, more generally, ideas arising from the unconscious mind. A time for reflection, quiet thought, and study may also be signified, especially if the Querent is taking up a new interest or hobby.

Reversed

Personality When reversed, this card may represent a lazy, frivolous person who neglects to use skills and talents. Despite a wide range of interests, this person fails to make a commitment to anything in particular, drifting from one activity to another and achieving little. There is much wasted potential here.

Situation The Querent has artistic, creative or psychic talents which are undeveloped at present. Alternatively, a potentially helpful aspect of the situation has been overlooked, possibly because the Querent is ignoring impressions coming from the unconscious mind.

Page of Swords

Personality This person is intelligent and discerning, quick to see to the heart of any matter, but also cautious and discreet when taking action. In making decisions, he or she is able to weigh up all the possibilities and alternatives, leading to sound and responsible judgement, and is helpful in resolving disputes. However, this cautious approach may be due to mistrust of others.

Situation The situation calls for alertness, clear thinking and intelligent decision-making. It is necessary to consider various options carefully and then act decisively. Caution and tact may also be needed, and the Querent should beware of someone intending harm.

Reversed

Personality This card represents a cunning, devious and hypocritical person who feels insecure and tries to protect him- or herself and gain an advantage by exploiting the weaknesses in others. This person is likely to use disputes between other people to further personal ends, encouraging enmity and bad feeling.

Situation The Querent may have good reason to believe that there are enemies present. Suspicion and caution could be justified in this situation, and it may be necessary to take precautions against the actions of unscrupulous people. However, being in an atmosphere of tension and mistrust for too long can be harmful in itself, so steps should be taken to resolve differences and to deal with troublemakers.

Page of Coins

Personality This card represents a hard-working, practical and dependable person, possibly a student, an apprentice, or someone in a junior position in business. Careful and methodical in approach, he or she is well-organised and good at administration and routine work, but can also be relied upon to take responsibility when necessary.

Situation The Querent may be engaged in activity of a routine nature where attention to detail is necessary. Although this can be boring, the situation is probably only temporary — perhaps because the Querent is training for a particular career, and there are prospects of promotion. Any dull, methodical activity may be indicated, but there are likely to be rewards in the long term if the Querent is patient.

Reversed

Personality This person is rather boring, slow and pompous, is envious and resentful of more intelligent people and likes to assert what little power he or she has in annoying and obstructive ways. This card can represent a minor official or clerical worker who causes delays and makes problems for the Querent.

Situation The Querent is engaged in boring activity or a tedious process which seems to bring no rewards. Trouble with bureaucracy may be indicated, or some other frustrating situation which is making the Querent feel tired and fed-up. Worries about money, or being bogged down by a monotonous lifestyle or job are possible interpretations.

The Knights

These cards are sometimes called Princes, but they usually depict men on horseback. In a reading, they represent young men, and sometimes situations in which movement, progress and activity in either a literal or metaphorical sense are important (as symbolised by the horse, which is a means of transport). All the Knights correspond to the element of fire, and the vitality of fire is a feature of the meanings of these cards, moderated according to the element of the suit to which each card belongs.

Knight of Wands

Personality A charming, witty and elegant young man is represented by this card. He is warm, generous and fun-loving, and his attractive personality brings him many friends. He is also adventurous and likes to try out new experiences, but he may have a tendency to be wild and unpredictable.

Situation Excitement and activity are indicated. This card often represents physical activities, travel, moving home, or going on holiday. It stands for adventure, and change for the better.

Reversed

Personality He is a wild, excitable and unreliable person who is inclined to make hasty judgements and act recklessly. His presence often causes chaos, and sometimes he stirs up trouble for the fun of it. He is impatient, abandoning projects before they are finished, and seeking sensation and instant success.

Situation The Querent is under stress and finding it hard to cope with changes happening now. The situation seems chaotic and confusing, and the Querent may be at odds with other people and their needs. Stressful travelling, too much physical activity, or an unwise move of home may be signified.

Knight of Cups

Personality He is a sensitive, imaginative and romantic young man who has original ideas, is inventive and idealistic. However, he is rather quiet and passive, and may be easily influenced by others, or inclined to indulge in fantasy rather than apply his ideas practically. His arrival may bring the Querent new opportunities — especially of a romantic nature.

Situation Romantic experiences, love, marriage, or a new personal relationship may be signified. New ideas and opportunities for creative and artistic pursuits can also be indicated.

Reversed

Personality This card may represent a person who is not as pleasant as he seems. His quiet and amiable manner may conceal secret motives, and he is not very truthful. This is probably not because he wants to hurt anyone, but because he is afraid of the consequences of telling the truth, and is trying to protect himself by seeming to be what he is not.

Situation There are unforeseen problems in a situation which appears favourable. The Querent may be deceived or in some way deluded, and is relying on false hopes. It may be necessary to face up to some unpleasant truths.

Knight of Swords

Personality The young man represented by this card is intelligent, courageous, and capable in a difficult situation. He confronts obstacles and opposition in an open and direct way, and is a good friend to have in times of trouble because he deals with problems swiftly and effectively. He may represent someone who will be a strong ally when the Querent needs help.

Situation This card tends to appear when the Querent faces difficulties and is likely to be in conflict with other people. However, in its upright position it indicates that opposition will be overcome and that the Querent will achieve the desired ends despite initial problems. A firm and rational approach is most likely to be effective.

Reversed

Personality He is an aggressive, impatient young man who puts a great deal of effort into his activities and yet achieves poor results because his approach is clumsy and blundering. He often finds himself in conflict with others, and wastes energy in coping with problems he has created by not planning ahead or thinking before he acts.

Situation Trouble is likely to arise, and an angry, confrontational attitude will only make matters worse. Impulsive action will lead to blunders and will later be regretted, so the Querent should plan carefully before proceeding. A calmer, more tactful approach is more likely to be effective.

Knight of Coins

Personality This young man is gentle, kind and dependable. He is not especially intelligent, but enjoys a quiet and simple life, and has a practical, hard-working and down-to-earth attitude. He may be rather slow at times, but with patient and steady application he usually achieves in the end what he set out to do.

Situation Life may seem rather slow at the moment, with few interesting or exciting things happening. The Querent should take the opportunity to relax and have a good time. Slow but steady progress will be made, and goals will be reached eventually.

Reversed

Personality A very dull, conservative person is represented when this card is reversed. He is slow and plodding in his approach, which seems inappropriate in the circumstances. He may be reluctant to abandon old ways of thinking and behaviour, even though they prove ineffective, and his way of life has become stuck in a rut.

Situation The Querent is making very little progress towards achieving what is desired. Matters seem to have slowed down almost to a standstill, and the situation looks boring and hopeless. A change of approach may be needed here to stimulate some action and to revive the Querent's interest in what is happening.

The Queens

Queens represent mature women. In a female Querent's spread, a Queen is likely to represent the Querent herself. All the Queens correspond to the feminine element of water, so their personalities are influenced by the qualities associated with this element. As we have already seen in the case of the Pages and Knights, however, the element associated with each suit also determines the personalities of these Court cards.

Queen of Wands

This card represents a woman with a sociable and outgoing personality who has a busy and active life. She is a capable person who can direct her energy into many different activities — both work and leisure pursuits. She is warm, sympathetic and generous, and has many friends. As a wife and mother she is loving and faithful, but she also makes a very efficient business woman, and has an independent mind.

Reversed

When reversed, this card represents someone who likes to see herself as efficient, organised and helpful, but who is inclined to interfere where she is not wanted. She likes to take over the running of things and thinks she knows best. She may be an over-protective mother, or generally someone who thinks that others cannot manage without her.

Queen of Cups

She is a quiet and gentle woman who conceals much of her personality and so has an air of mystery about her. She may appear to be a dreamer, but she has hidden strengths and her intuitive, artistic and psychic skills are likely to be highly developed. She is sensitive to the needs of others, and receptive to the promptings of her own unconscious mind.

She may seem a rather strange woman whose deep personality is difficult to understand, but she is creative, kind and sympathetic.

Reversed

In her reverse aspect she is a fickle and frivolous woman who is impractical and inclined to indulge in fantasy. A rather vain and silly person, she may appear attractive and so lure into trouble people who trust her, and then desert them because she is thinking only of her own interests. She does not have a very clear perception of reality and may be deceiving herself in some respects. Generally she is unstable and unreliable.

Queen of Swords

This woman is intelligent, independent and strong-willed. Traditionally the card represents a widow, but it can also represent a woman living alone because she is divorced or separated, or because she prefers independence. She may be a very ambitious person who values her career more than marriage and motherhood and so has remained single.

However, despite her strength and independence, the Queen of Swords can also be a lonely woman who sometimes experiences a sense of loss and who feels the need of companionship.

Reversed

She is an intelligent and ambitious woman who is inclined to further her own schemes at the expense of other people. She may be someone in a position of authority who enjoys the power she has over others. Cold, stern, critical and domineering, she seems incapable of any warm feelings, and is motivated by her own selfish desires. This cold exterior may conceal an inner loneliness, however. Possibly she is someone who has been hurt deeply, and now harbours a grudge or feelings of bitterness and resentment, so that her apparent insensitivity is a form of self-defence.

Queen of Coins

This woman is sensuous, warm and affectionate. She is a home-loving person who creates a pleasant and cosy atmosphere around her. She makes a caring wife and mother, and is also fond of entertaining because she is generous and likes to have fun, and she is happiest when she can share what she has with others. She is a practical, sensible person who appreciates beautiful things and is probably a nature-lover.

Reversed

In her reverse aspect she is someone who is over-concerned with material things and who likes to show off her possessions and social status. She may worry about what the neighbours think, put on airs and graces and behave in a suspicious and jealous manner. Sometimes she will complain about her misfortunes, because underneath her pretensions she is an insecure person who feels unloved, and much of her unpleasant behaviour may be a way of seeking attention.

The Kings

Kings (sometimes called Princes) represent mature men. If the Querent is male, a King in the spread may represent the Querent's own personality. All the Kings stand for the masculine element of air, and so possess the rationality and authority associated with that element, combined with the qualities of the element associated with the particular suit to which each King belongs.

King of Wands

This man is accomplished, responsible, and has a confident and optimistic attitude. He is strong-willed, but also very fair-minded and able to appreciate other people's points of view, so he is good at giving unbiased advice and resolving disputes.

He is enthusiastic, energetic, charming and witty, though inclined to be impatient with detail. Dependable and affectionate, he is a good husband and father, and generous to people he knows. He often has good ideas and is resourceful and enterprising.

Reversed

He is an intolerant person who is critical of other people's faults but fails to recognise his own. He likes to believe that he always knows best, and expects others to fit in with his own requirements. He may be inclined to moralise because he thinks he has higher standards than most people, but his attitude comes across as narrow-minded and perhaps even hypocritical. He is unsympathetic and patronising, believing that he is advising people for their own good, while failing to listen to them or to respond to their real needs.

King of Cups

This card usually represents a cultured and sophisticated man who is intelligent and well-educated. He may be a professional person such as a doctor, solicitor, or business colleague, as he is someone whose personal and deeper feelings are concealed from the Querent and who seems somewhat cool and aloof. On the other hand, this coolness may be part of his personality. He may be someone who finds it hard to express emotion and who is embarrassed by intimacy, but this reserve can cause problems in close relationships.

He is an honest and caring person, but he may be difficult to understand and is perhaps not even in touch with his own feelings, so although he is supportive to those he loves, he is slow to demonstrate affection.

Reversed

When reversed, this card represents a man who appears elegant and sophisticated but who cannot be trusted. He conceals his real motives and is scheming and unscrupulous, using his superior intelligence, education, and privileged social contacts, to take advantage of others. He may be a professional person or business associate of whom the Querent should beware. On the other hand, he could be someone in the Querent's private life who is deceiving them, lying or cheating, while appearing suave and respectable on the surface.

King of Swords

This is an intelligent and powerful man who likes to be in a position of authority. He is independent, and dislikes restrictions of any kind being placed upon him, which may include personal ties, other people's preferences, or a traditional way of doing things. He prefers to be innovatory and to try out new ideas, and favours all things modern.

He is ambitious, rational and assertive, and is most successful in situations where these qualities are required. He may represent a professional person who will be of help to the Querent, especially with regard to business and legal matters.

Reversed

The reverse aspects of this personality are most unpleasant. The card is likely to represent a selfish and domineering man who exploits people weaker than himself. He is intelligent, aggressive, and heedless of the feelings of others, and he can be extremely unkind or even cruel. He may be someone who has the power to manipulate or bully the Querent, but he is a dangerous person to know and his company is best avoided.

King of Coins

This card represents a kind, good-natured man who is successful and contented. He is practical and hard-working, and has achieved stability and security in his life as a result of his own efforts. This security may include material wealth which is the reward for his labours, though he never seeks money for its own sake, and is always ready to share what he has with others.

He is a plain and simple man who enjoys the good things in life and has much common sense, though he is not especially intelligent. He may be a skilled craftsman or someone who enjoys making things with his hands, for his gifts are of a practical rather than an intellectual nature.

Reversed

He is a weak person who has become preoccupied with money and material security. He is likely to be dull, rather stupid and insensitive, and unable to appreciate the finer things in life. His relationships may have suffered as a result of his greedy and miserly attitude, but this has only increased his desire to seek pleasure in material things which can give him no real satisfaction.

He is an unhappy person, obstinate and resistant to change, who may take out his frustrations on other people, and who has lost sight of the things of real value in his life.

CHAPTER SIX

OTHER USES OF
THE TAROT

Although the Tarot is chiefly known as a form of divination, it can be used for other purposes as well. As already mentioned in Chapter 2, a Tarot reading, in any case, is not purely predicting the future. Readings done for other people can often take the form of counselling, while those done for oneself may be a type of meditation. In this chapter we shall look at the use of Tarot for both purposes, as well as for story-telling.

Meditation

Meditation on the images of the Major Arcana is sometimes recommended as a way of learning about the meanings of the cards for the purpose of divination. However, it can also be employed in magical training, or as a way of discovering the archetypes represented by the cards within one's own psyche. Meditation on a Tarot image can be revealing in the way that dreams are revealing, providing insights from the unconscious mind.

It is sometimes said that the cards of the Major Arcana should be studied in the sequence in which they are numbered, starting with

The Fool and ending with The World, because the Major Arcana is designed to be a psychic journey and each card represents a stage of the journey which would be confusing if it were experienced out of the proper sequence. However, those who attribute the cards to paths on the Cabala's Tree of Life will have a different idea of the order in which they should be studied; while those who are using meditation on the Major Arcana as a form of self-counselling (as described in the next section) may follow yet another sequence of the cards. It is really a matter of personal choice which card you meditate upon first, though for obvious reasons it may not be a good idea to start with cards such as The Devil or The Tower, as you will probably have more negative thoughts and feelings about them.

When you are going to meditate, ensure that you are in a quiet room without distractions, and that you are unlikely to be disturbed. It may be helpful to play a tape of relaxing, mood-enhancing music, although some people find this a distraction. Study for a while the card which you have chosen to meditate upon. When you have fixed the picture in your memory, dim the lighting, or draw the curtains, and sit in a comfortable chair.

Close your eyes and, first, concentrate on relaxing your body. If you know techniques for relaxation or self-hypnosis, you might like to use these. A simple method is to concentrate on each part of the body in turn, starting with the feet, and to release any tension from the muscles.

When you have done this, start to visualise the Tarot card which you have chosen. When you can see it clearly in your mind's eye, imagine it growing larger, until the scene and figures depicted appear life-size. Next, see this image not as a two-dimensional card, but as a three-dimensional scene, as if viewed through a doorway, with the edges of the card forming the door frame and the threshold. Concentrate for a while, until the scene seems as real as you can make it, and then imagine that you are stepping through the doorway, into the landscape of the Tarot card.

While you are there, you may have a variety of experiences. The characters may move about and speak to you; or you may ask them questions, walk around in the imaginary landscape and explore other features of it for yourself. The duration of the experience may be brief or prolonged, and likewise its quality could be anything from trivial to profound. The first few attempts may be disappointing, as it can be hard for beginners to sustain a visualisation clearly, making it difficult for some people to imagine the initial stage of stepping inside the Tarot card. Once this has been achieved, however, the process of meditation becomes easier with practice.

When the meditation is over, imagine that you are stepping back out through the doorway by which you entered. If you have moved to another place in the landscape, or the original doorway has vanished, visualise a doorway back into the world of everyday waking consciousness, and step through it. Failing to do this is not dangerous, but it is undesirable. Opening your eyes suddenly and jumping up can be disturbing and disorienting after you have been in a state of deep relaxation, as in hypnosis, where an altered state of consciousness is attained. Also, unless you perform some ritual procedure in the imagination to end the meditation, the unconscious mind will tend to behave as if you are still meditating, causing unwanted thoughts and images to intrude on your other activities for several hours afterwards.

It is useful to write down, immediately after the meditation, as much of the experience as you can remember, for future reference, even if it seems silly or trivial, or if very little happened at all. As with a dream, the significance of what occurred may become apparent later on, or new insights about it may be gained after subsequent meditation sessions.

Counselling

The Tarot may be used in a number of different ways in counselling. Some professional Tarot readers use a counselling approach, rather than clairvoyance or prediction. In divination where clairvoyance is used, the Querent usually takes a fairly passive role, while the reader makes predictions. When the counselling approach is used, on the other hand, the reader comments on the cards in a such a way as to stimulate the Querent's own thoughts and feelings. The Querent is encouraged to talk about personal feelings and about his or her response to the cards and to the reader's interpretation. In a reading of this nature, the Querent may do most of the talking, while the reader, rather than giving advice or opinions, guides the Querent towards finding personal answers to the problems which need to be resolved in the reading.

As you will see from the sample readings in Chapter 2, our own method tends towards counselling, but this does not mean that we consider counselling superior to clairvoyance. They are both equally valid methods, and many Tarot readers use a combination of the two, or vary their approach according to the needs of the individual Querent.

Robert Wang's *Tarot Psychology* book and Tarot card set is designed specifically for use in counselling. The cards are based on Jungian psychology, and may be used by a professional therapist as diagnostic tools for arousing associations in the mind of the patient. Wang also describes how the cards may be used in a programme of self-therapy in which they are meditated upon in a manner similar to that described above, in the section on meditation.

Story-Telling

Within a group or psychic circle, Tarot cards may be used for story-telling, either as an end in itself, or as a form of guided meditation or group counselling. Each person may bring his or her own Tarot deck, or one deck may be kept especially for group work, to be used by the group as a whole.

Each person chooses a card at random, and some time is allowed for people to study their chosen cards before anyone starts to speak. Taking turns, each individual comments on his or her own card, expressing feelings, impressions and ideas about it, perhaps by inventing a fantasy based on the card's image, relating the picture to a personal experience, or simply expressing ideas that the picture suggests. After each person has finished speaking, the group may comment on what has been said, with the aim of being helpful and supportive, rather than criticising in a negative way.

An alternative method is for each person to comment on a card chosen on the basis of its appeal or some personal significance, instead of making the selection at random.

When using the cards in guided meditation, one member of the group leads the others in the meditation, which is based on a single Tarot card or sequence of cards. The participants sit or lie in comfortable positions while the leader instructs them stage by stage in a relaxation procedure and takes them on a journey of the imagination, describing the scenes and characters which they are to visualise. At the end, they should be brought back to everyday consciousness in the same way as in private meditation.

A group may also use Tarot cards for a kind of story-telling game. Each person picks a card at random from a single deck. One person starts a story based on his or her chosen card, and the other people take turns in continuing the story in a way suggested by their own cards.

Some professional authors use Tarot cards to help in developing plots for novels. Occasionally this is apparent in the finished result. Italo Calvino's novel, *The Castle of Crossed Destinies* is a collection of interrelated short stories based on sequences of Tarot cards, set within a framing story in which the characters are unable to speak to one another and can communicate only by means of telling stories with the cards.

We used a similar technique to write a fantasy novel called *The Faceless Tarot* (Seddon and Almond, 1989). Cards were selected at random and used to devise a plot, each chapter being based on an individual card. This structure was allowed to remain visible in the finished novel, since the story was about a magician using Tarot cards, and so the same cards featured overtly in the plot. This need not be the case, however, for some writers use Tarot cards to inspire ideas without their stories being about the Tarot.

These are a few of the various uses to which Tarot may be put. Some of them are closely related to Tarot as a form of divination, while others are more like playing a game. In this book it is possible to mention such uses only briefly. Books which examine these aspects of the Tarot in greater depth, or from the point of view of using the cards primarily for purposes other than divination, are those by Alfred Douglas, Sallie Nichols, Emily Peach, Ellen Cannon Reed, Juliet Sharman-Burke (1989), Barbara Walker (1990), Robert Wang (1988), and Gerd Ziegler, which we have included in the bibliography at the end of this book.

SELECT BIBLIOGRAPHY

Almond, J. and Seddon K., *Tarot for Relationships*, Aquarian Press, Wellingborough (1990).

Calvino, Italo, *The Castle of Crossed Destinies*, Secker & Warburg, London (1977).

Cavendish, Richard, *The Tarot*, Michael Joseph, London (1975).

Crowley, Aleister, *The Book of Thoth*, Samuel Weiser, York Beach, Maine (1969).

Crowley, Vivianne, *Wicca: The Old Religion in the New Age*, Aquarian Press, Wellingborough (1989).

Douglas, Alfred, *The Tarot*, Penguin, Harmondsworth (1973).

Gilchrist, Cherry, *Divination: the Search for Meaning*, Dryad Press, London (1987).

Jung, C.G., *Man and His Symbols*, Aldus Books, London (1964).

Hamilton, E. and Cairns, H. (eds), *Plato: The Collected Dialogues*, Princeton University Press, Princeton, New Jersey (1961).

Huson, Paul, *The Devil's Picturebook*, Abacus, London (1972).

Lurker, Manfred, *Dictionary of Gods and Goddesses, Devils and Demons*, Routledge & Kegan Paul, London (1987).

Nichols, Sallie, *Jung and Tarot*, Samuel Weiser, York Beach, Maine (1984).

Noble, Vicki, *Motherpeace*, Harper & Rowe, San Francisco (1983).

Peach, Emily, *The Tarot Workbook*, Aquarian Press, Wellingborough (1984).

Pollack, Rachel, *Seventy-Eight Degrees of Wisdom* [2 vols], Aquarian Press, Wellingborough (1984).

Reed, Ellen Cannon, *The Witches Tarot*, Llewellyn Publications, St Paul, Minnesota (1989).

Seddon, K. and Almond, J., *The Faceless Tarot*, Dunscaith Publishing, London (1989).

Sharman-Burke, Juliet, *The Complete Book of Tarot*, Pan Books, London (1985).

Sharman-Burke, J. and Greene, L., *The Mythic Tarot*, Century Hutchinson, London (1986).

—— , *The Mythic Tarot Workbook*, Rider, London (1989).

Waite, A.E., *The Pictorial Key to the Tarot*, Rider, London (1971).

Walker, Barbara G., *The Secrets of the Tarot*, Harper & Row, San Francisco (1985).

SELECT BIBLIOGRAPHY

———, *Women's Rituals*, Harper & Row, San Francisco (1990).

Wang, Robert, *An Introduction to the Golden Dawn Tarot*, Aquarian Press, Wellingborough (1978).

———, *Tarot Psychology*, Urania Verlags AG, Neuhausen, Germany (1988).

Warner, Marina, *Monuments and Maidens*, Picador, London (1985).

Woudhuysen, Jan, *Tarotmania*, Wildwood House, London (1979).

Ziegler, Gerd, *Tarot: Mirror of the Soul*, Samuel Weiser, Maine (1988).

INDEX

INDEX

INDEX